The Soul of Western Civilization
Western Law from the Ancient Greeks to Today

By Joseph DiRienzo, M.A.

Author: Joseph DiRienzo, M.A.
Cover Designer: germancreative (fiverr.com/germancreative)
Editor: Jessica Lopez (fiverr.com/writerjessica22)
Published using KDP

Table of Contents

Dedication

I dedicate this book to God, the Creator of all things and our Father and Brother. Law is a reflection of God's natural and supernatural order. For His grace, I am eternally grateful.

***

"We have no government armed with power capable of contending with human passions unbridled by morality and religion. Our Constitution was made only for a moral and religious people. It is wholly inadequate to the government of any other." - John Adams

"And can the liberties of a nation be thought secure when we have removed their only firm basis, a conviction in the minds of the people that these liberties are of the gift of God? That they are not to be violated but with His wrath? Indeed I tremble for my country when I reflect that God is just; that his justice cannot sleep forever." -Thomas Jefferson

"The laws of nature are but the mathematical thoughts of God."- Euclid

"The only stable state is the one in which all men are equal before the law." - Aristotle

"No one is free who does not lord over himself." - Claudius Caesar

"For there is but one essential justice which cements society, and one law which establishes this justice. This law is right reason, which is the true rule of all commandments and prohibitions. Whoever neglects this law, whether written or unwritten, is necessarily unjust and wicked." – Cicero

Acknowledgements

Writing and compiling a monograph is no simple task without the support and help of many wonderful family members and friends. First and foremost, I thank my wife, Melissa, and my children, Mary Louise and Michael James, for their ongoing love and support for me to chase my dreams of higher education and historical research. Among our regular responsibilities of work, school and family I was afforded the time to attend to scholarship, research and writing.

Thanks to my family, especially: my loving mom Mary, my deceased father James A., my mentor and brother James, and my dear aunts Concetta Angelino, Paula Sanfilippo, and Joyce Anzalone; for being the greatest cheerleaders, role models and loving examples of faith, hard work, intellectual pursuit and simple kindness.

I give a special "thank you" to my editor, Jessica Lopez, who is an amazing writer and reviewer. Quite simply, I could not have completed this work without her insight and collaboration.

There are several dear friends who believed in me and supported my endeavors throughout my life, in good times and bad. I will be forever grateful for their love, confidence and support.

Personal Note to the Reader

"Wondrously strange then, and much to be regretted indeed would it be, were we to neglect the means, and to stray from the road to which the finger of Providence has so manifestly pointed. I cannot believe it will ever come to pass! The great Author of all good has not conducted us so far on the road to happiness and glory to withdraw from us, in the hour of need, his beneficent support. By folly and misconduct (proceeding from a variety of causes) we may now and then get bewildered; but I hope, and trust, that there is good sense and virtue enough left to bring us back into the right way before we shall be entirely lost."

- George Washington, in a letter to Benjamin Lincoln, June 29, 1788

A society is nothing apart from the culmination of its soul: its collective aspirations, beliefs, customs, ethics and principles as encoded in its laws. George Washington's exclamation, "…it will never come to pass," is salted with an admonition about a just society should it falter: "We shall be entirely lost."

In the author's humble opinion, the United States' Constitution is the crowning achievement of Western Civilization. The definition of Western Civilization continues to be the subject of lively, visceral, and at times excoriating debate throughout the centuries. Whatever your view, it cannot be denied that Western Civilization has been a catalyst for unprecedented human rights and freedom. Before you react to that statement I ask that you continue to read.

This is written during a time when Western Civilization is being repudiated for its history, both recent and past. In the United States there is a resurgence of iconoclastic activity, including the removal of historical figures from centers of learning and the like. The founders of America's Constitution are being upbraided rather anachronistically, not for their beliefs for which they risked "our lives, our fortunes and our sacred honor" by signing the Declaration of Independence, but for what some of them practiced during an age when slavery was ubiquitous.

1

This age had not only slavery, but indentured servitude, workhouses, and debtors' prisons which are entirely overlooked. It was a harsh time for sure.

As such, these prominent, wealthy and well-educated men of privilege, after studying Western Civilization and its millennia of growth, had a deep understanding of the effects that geopolitical institutions, social conditions, intellectual foundations, economics and religion have on a society. These men are now criticized for being the last in a legacy of the so-called patriarchy.

While no human conventions are perfect, the laws of Western Civilization have afforded modern civilization with the unparalleled freedom to stray from the "road to happiness" and become "bewildered". The challenge of our time is: do we have enough "good sense and virtue to bring us back into the right way before we shall be entirely lost"?

The following is a gathering of the author's historical research papers dedicated to rediscovering the origins of Western Law. They are arranged in order, following the Ancient Greeks, Ancient Romans, Byzantines, the Renaissance and Reformation eras of Western Europe, and culminating in the United States of America. Each successive society and their lawgivers contributed its own experiences and beliefs to the body of law we now view as Western Law.

It is the author's wish that this work provides readers with a rudimentary background and understanding of the development of Western Law and its fundamental and priceless underpinning of Western Civilization; and that it opens up a new interest in the historical study and pleasure reading of Western Law for future generations seeking a society blessed by the time-honored 'Rule of the Law', as Aristotle advises:

"Wherefore it is thought to be just that among equals everyone be ruled as well as rule, and therefore that any should have their turn. We thus arrive at law; for an order of succession implies law. And the **rule of the law**, it is argued, is preferable to that of any individual. On the same principle, even if it be better for certain individuals to govern, they should be made only guardians and ministers of the law." - Aristotle, *Politics,* Book III, Part XVI

Best Regards,
Joseph DiRienzo
June 11, 2019

Chapter I

Ancient Greece and the Development of Western Democratic Thought, Economics and Governance

Historiography

Introduction

During the 5th Century BCE, Athens and Sparta were the most prominent city-states on the Greek mainland. At that time Greece was comprised of several individual *poleis (polis* singular*)*, or what are loosely defined today as city-states. As such, Athens and Sparta were Ancient Greek city-states that were sovereign territories. Despite this common status, each *polis* had distinct differences politically, militarily, culturally and socially. Tragically, these city-states would collide in the Peloponnesian War, fought between Athens and Sparta that had long-lasting and devastating effects on Ancient Greece that redefined its culture and future.

1. Greek Historians

Herodotus (484 – 425 BCE) is widely thought of as the father of history in the sense that prior to Herodotus historical accounts were oral and passed down through the generations. Herodotus made an effort to write down these accounts and shed light on the past in as neutral a manner as possible. His work *The Histories* looks back over 100 years into Ancient Greece's past to part of their later Archaic period. Following Herodotus were several Greek historians such as Thucydides (472 – 400 BCE), Xenophon (431 – 354 BCE) and Demosthenes (384 – 322 BCE). Most of them were from Athens or their works promoted Athens, which helped preserve the historical record regarding Athens over other *poleis*. Their primary focus was on political, military and diplomatic life as many of them were statesmen and military leaders. As a result, not as much information exists regarding economic and social issues, and Sparta was also overlooked in the same manner.

Other notable historians of Ancient Greece include John Gillies (1747 – 1836 CE), a Scottish historian who wrote the *History of Ancient Greece* in 1786, where he criticized democracy and argued for a stronger monarchical structure; George Grote (1794 – 1871), an English historian known for his book the *History of Greece* that shared a radical political perspective during the revolutionary periods of America and France; and Karl Julius Beloch (1854 – 1929), a German scholar who was known for his skepticism of sources and often redefined the meaning of how such events were relayed.

Modern historians include Donald Kagan (b. 1932), an American history scholar who has written extensively on Ancient Greece in his work *The Peloponnesian War* in 2003, and Luciano Canfora (b. 1942), an Italian historian whose recent work *Democracy in Europe* (2006) maps Western democracy back to the Ancient Greek civilization.

2. Ancient Greece: A Gathering of City-States

The Ancient Greek world was mostly comprised of a fragile, distrustful conglomeration of *poleis* or city-states, influenced and caught between the Ancient Eastern and Western civilizations. In the east were the Persians located in what is modern-day Iran and their satellites. In the west were the Greek city-states. Chief among them were Athens, located in Southeastern Greece on the Aegean Sea on a small peninsula known as Attica, and Sparta, which was ensconced deep within a much larger peninsula further west in Southern Greece known as Peloponnese. These geographic distinctions are important because both Athens' and Sparta's geographic locations played major roles in the causes leading to the pyrrhic Peloponnesian War, how it was conducted and its ultimate conclusion; a conclusion that transformed Ancient Greece forever.

3. Sparta & Athens

Sparta had a constitutional government and maintained a dual kingship handed down from father to son. They also had a Senate which was essentially an oligarchy controlled by a few wealthy families and five *ephors,* who were the city-state's civil leaders. Spartan virtues are famous and include: abstinence, toughness, self-discipline, civic patriotism, loyalty to friends, justice in economic dealings and extreme piety among others. They had a strong military society where order was considered the highest of duties.

6

Spartan society followed defined rites of passage and education for its citizens as the basis for its austere lifestyle. Sparta observed many festivals in celebration of their rituals and social customs. These festivals began at youth and carried on throughout their lives. The festivals celebrated their physical and educational training. This way of life permeated the Spartan consciousness and manifested itself in its internal and external geopolitical policies. Spartans perceived themselves as the rightful leaders of the Ancient Greek civilization.

Athenian society was built on the rule of law and a concept of equal rights for all citizens - the origins of democracy   Athens was the civic center of the Athenians' life. Citizens worked both in the city and throughout the countryside farming or performing city labor. Athenians were united by their self-governance; they defended their city-state, supplied goods and worshiped the gods together as fundamental underpinnings of their society. They attributed much of their success to their navy (which Athens prided itself on creating), their city-state's patriotism, the Athenian leadership and its courage in battle against a superior enemy.

4. The Peloponnesian War

It is impossible to discuss Athens and Sparta without including the Peloponnesian War. While warfare molded both Sparta and Athens, after the Persian Wars there was instantly a sizeable rift between the two city-states. This devastating war redefined Athens and Sparta and doomed Ancient Greece to a fate they surely did not desire.

For good reason, the Ancient Greek Theater is noted for its famous tragedies. The Ancient Greeks evolved out of a storied past filled with remarkable successes and significant tragedies much like those relayed in Homer's *Iliad* and *Odyssey*, complete with heroes, villains (or 'protagonists' as the Greeks referred to them) and their instructive consequences. The Peloponnesian War fought between Athens and Sparta was one such tragedy, or series of tragedies, not acted out in an Ancient Greek amphitheater, but across Ancient Greece itself and had monumental consequences on their culture, geopolitics and civilization.

7

To set our tragedian stage, in the years prior to the Peloponnesian War, the Ancient Greek city-states had forged an alliance against a common enemy: the Persians. The Persian Wars (499 - 449 BCE) were fought between the Persian Empire and the allied city-states of Ancient Greece. Persia's hegemony included designs on conquering the significant city-states of Ancient Greece mainly in the east, but would eventually include Athens in the west. Beginning with the conquest of Ionia in 547 BCE, Ancient Greece would be plagued with concerns regarding Persian aggression and expansion. Persia was in the habit of appointing tyrants to its satellites and this did not sit well with the free-minded Greeks. Ancient Greeks, by heritage, were a free-thinking people and resisted all forms of external and internal domination. The Ionians would, in time, revolt unsuccessfully against the Persians with the help of Athens. This action would enflame the Persians who would subsequently include Athens as part of their retribution for supporting Ionia's revolt. The Persian plan was to conquer Greece and make Athens pay for its insolence.

In 490 BCE, the Persians sent an expeditionary naval force across the Aegean Sea initially capturing the islands of the Cyclades and destroying Eretria on Euboea in a push towards conquering Athens. This action prompted one of the most monumental rallying points for the Ancient Greek city-states during the Persian Wars.

Soon after the destruction of Eretria, the Persian navy would sail toward Attica and land its forces in a bay near the city of Marathon on the Greek mainland. Athens, with the help of nearby Plataea, deployed its hoplite forces to Marathon to meet the Persians in battle. In an historic military maneuver, the Athenians drew in the superior Persian forces and routed them. Much like an Ancient Greek tragedy, when the hour was darkest, the Greeks triumphed in what would become a turning point in their defense of the Greek homeland and in the psychology of Ancient Greeks. The Battle of Marathon became a rallying point, showing the Ancient Greeks that together they could be strong and ultimately defeat or push back the superior Persian forces. As obedient worshippers of the gods, they saw such a success as an endorsement of their civilization and its culture by the gods.

While this was a setback for the Persians, it would only further fuel their resentment for the Athenians. After a period of delay, the Persians would assemble an even larger military force with the intent to crush the Greeks and destroy Athens. In 480 BCE, the Persians marched a massive land force across hundreds of miles through Thrace and Macedonia to attack the Greeks from the north, while simultaneously sending a vast naval force across the Aegean Sea. The Greeks responded by assembling a significant military force which now included additional city-states, the most important being Sparta. Sparta's combat culture and martial prowess was widely recognized and the allied forces fell under their leadership. The land force met the Persians in an area known as Thermopylae. After a battle consisting of vastly outnumbered Greek forces, the Persians, after suffering disproportionate losses, won the Battle of Thermopylae. However, it did not serve as a decisive victory for the Persians and further rallied the Greeks.

The Greek naval forces fared better, in that much of the Persian fleet was destroyed in the unpredictable weather on the Aegean Sea. In two subsequent battles, the Persian fleet was defeated. At the Battle of Artemisium (480 BCE), the Persians were unable to defeat the Ancient Greek fleet; but facing a greater force, the Greeks fell back to Salamis. It was at Salamis that the Persian fleet was outmaneuvered by the smaller, but more responsive Greek ships. The Greeks captured many Persian ships and won the Battle of Salamis (480 BCE), significantly weakening the Persian expeditionary forces and preventing a full scale invasion of the Peloponnese. Later, in 479 BCE, the Persians lost the final decisive land battle at Plataea.

The Greeks reassembled after their losses at Thermopylae, but holding back the Persians at Salamis, issued a large land force and met the Persians in their encampment at Plataea, northwest of Athens near the Peloponnese Peninsula. For the first time since the beginning of the Persian attacks, the Greeks faced them with nearly equal forces. The Persians, seeking a quick and decisive victory, underestimated the Greeks. As the Greeks were pulling back to strengthen their supply lines, the Persians assaulted them thinking they were retreating. This was a monumental error. The Greeks held their positions, inflicted heavy casualties on the Persians and killed the Persian commander. The

Battle of Plataea ultimately halted the Persian incursion into the Greek mainland and forced them to retreat back to their homelands.

As evidenced here, the allied Greek city-states realized their formidable power as allies in the face of a daunting enemy. The success of the Persian Wars and subsequent expulsion of remaining Persian forces from the Ancient Greek sphere gave the Ancient Greeks an enormous emotional and psychological boost to their collective self-image and bolstered the belief that they were favored by the gods for their choices and actions as a civilization.

With regard to the geopolitics of Ancient Greece, the Persian Wars gave the city-states cause for creating a more permanent alliance, and as a result, one of the major outcomes was Athens' ascension among the Greek city-states to leadership status and the creation of the Delian League. The Delian League was comprised of approximately 150 Greek *poleis*, mainly from the east located around the Aegean Sea and Adriatic Sea, but did not include those located on the Peloponnese, who remained in Sparta's long-standing Peloponnesian League.

After the Persian Wars Sparta, who led the defense forces with its Peloponnesian League partners, believed that the fragile alliance was unsustainable, and since the Persians were repulsed, there was no need to maintain an additional alliance unless future need arose. Athens disagreed with Sparta and immediately assumed leadership of this new alliance, called the Delian League because its finances were held on the island of Delos. The Delian League's purpose was to prepare for any imminent invasions of Greece. Members would either send military forces or pay a tax to the Delian League. Most city-states agreed to pay the tax. Sparta felt very secure returning to its smaller circle of allies prior to the Persian Wars, mainly Corinth and Elis on the Peloponnese. This alliance is now known as the Peloponnesian League. Sparta was uncomfortable not being the dominant leader of their alliances and was already the sole leader of the Peloponnesian League. The fact that the Delian League was led by Athens made the Spartans even more uneasy. This would signal the beginning of a new phase of conflict in Ancient Greece: a civil conflict between the two dominant city-states (Sparta and Athens) and their allies after the Persian Wars.

The combination of Spartan virtues, its martial focus and its top-down governance made for a militaristic, controlled society. Despite its constitutional government, Spartan society relied heavily on a slave population called the helots. The helots were largely farmers who supported the Spartan city-state and were cruelly treated. Spartans were used to helot revolts and were utterly distrustful and fearful of them. Sparta, unlike its neighboring city-states in Ancient Greece, acquired needed space for its growing populations not by colonizing, but by conquering; as witnessed in the Messenia Wars in the 8th, 7th and 4th centuries BCE, where whole populations were reduced to helot status under Spartan control.

Despite their military superiority, Sparta was hesitant to make war with external forces because of their internal need to govern and control the helots. Sparta led an affiliation of local city-states in an alliance as mentioned before, called the Peloponnesian League, which mainly concentrated on Peloponnese concerns. The combination of their superior military position, an austere society poised for leadership, and their interest in protecting Peloponnese's self-interests, positioned Sparta to resist Athenian supremacy at all costs.

Out of distrust for Athens, Sparta resisted Athens' desire to rebuild its fortifications after the Persians razed them during the war. In this, Sparta tried to reduce Athens' strength. The Athenians were resentful of Sparta for this. The Spartans considered a proposal to declare war on Athens, depose the Delian League and commandeer its navy to submit to Spartan control. It was clear after the Persian Wars that a clash between these two city-states was imminent.

With the military success of the Persian Wars, the institution of the Delian League with Athens as its hegemony, Athens viewed itself more an empire than a city-state. An Athenian envoy's speech to the Spartan Congress in 432 BCE was bold, in that Athens asserted its power and hailed its role in the Persian Wars as crucial to its successful outcome despite Spartan involvement. It was not only a plea to Sparta to not break its oaths of peace, but a petition countered with Athens' warning to fight them should Sparta seek to do so first. It was clear in this speech that Athens felt it was rightfully an empire and had no cause to back

11

away from its imperial expansion. This did not sit well with the Spartans and ultimately provoked their increased ire for Athens.

What is interesting about this overconfident speech is that it points to several strengths and weaknesses in Athens' self-examination. Athens considered its leadership as enlightened and approved by the gods for their successes in war, notably the victories at Marathon and Salamis against the Persians. They attributed much of the success to their navy, their city-state's patriotism, the Athenian leadership and its courage in battle against a superior enemy. They considered Sparta late in their engagement of the Persians. Athens exhibits self-confidence that they were preordained to handle the responsibility of leadership and empire given the circumstances. They perceived that Athens was the ablest city-state to lead the empire, enacting their leadership with the justice they lived by in their city-state.

This outlook was strengthened because Athens was experiencing unprecedented prosperity, population growth, wealth and the laurels of military victory in an extraordinary cultural explosion. Athens developed spectacles of the theater in their comedies and tragedies, and under Pericles they invested in monumental works of art and architecture, as in the Parthenon and other structures of the Acropolis. A vast array of thinkers examined the use of human reason to understand and pursue developments in the disciplines of law, moral code, and politics, the natural, medical and social sciences and literature, all still holding relevance today. Athens' hegemony was obviously projected through its domination of the Delian League, but its most important influence was that of its democratic principles.

It may come as a surprise to modern readers that some assert that it was the need for military defense that caused democracy to begin. The Greek *polis* conscripted most of its male citizens as armed defenders called the hoplites. Hoplites were citizen-soldiers. It seems that the impetus for citizens to rally and defend their city provided a significant opportunity to meet, speak of common concerns, and work to address and resolve such issues once service was completed; but while this was fostering the right environment for democratic ideals, this was not the sole reason for their development. Athenian society was built on the rule of law and a concept of equal rights for all citizens. The other Greek city-states were greatly influenced by these dynamics.

A second umbrage occurred when, despite Sparta's alliance with Thasos against Athens, Athens - under Cimon (510 - 450 BCE), the respected Athenian statesman and general - issued several thousand hoplites to assist Sparta after a major earthquake impacted the Laconia region on the Peloponnese, causing a helot revolt; but they were turned away. The gesture of offering assistance in times of need was common in Ancient Greece. In this instance, the Spartans accepted other city-state's assistance but not Athens'. This was an obvious slight. Thucydides perceived that the Spartan motive was because they believed that in the chaos, the Athenians would be motivated to side with the helots.

The Athenian reaction was immediate and intense. Cimon was ostracized from Athens for ten years as a result of the affront and because of his pro-Spartan policies. Cimon was the son of Miltiades, the victor of Marathon. This action against a man of Cimon's stature indicates the venom that the Athenian assembly had for Sparta. This would spur certain anti-Spartan factions to gain control and exhibit their animosity openly. Consequently, the Athenian assembly quickly made an alliance with Argos, a long-time enemy of Sparta.

After the helot revolt was suppressed by Sparta, they exiled the remaining helots involved. Athens stepped in to allow the exiles to inhabit Athens' newly acquired city of Naupactus, located on the Corinthian Gulf. At the same time, two city-states on the Peloponnese allied with Sparta: Megara and Corinth, who were fighting over a border dispute with Megara suffering defeat. Not choosing sides, Sparta caused Megara to threaten breaking their alliance and seeking support from Athens. Athens saw this as a vital, strategic opportunity, because Megara was located on Athens' western border between itself and the Peloponnesian city-states. It also gave speedier access for trade in the Corinthian Gulf, which previously required a treacherous voyage completely around the Peloponnese. The Spartans took great offense with Athens' actions in what they considered to be Sparta's backyard. These actions presaged a global tragedy for the Ancient Greek world and their civilization.

The Peloponnesian War is historically viewed as having two distinct phases known as the First and Second Peloponnesian Wars. The actions outlined above led to the First Peloponnesian War (460 – 445 BCE) which lasted fifteen years. During the struggle Sparta and Athens, mainly through allied city-states, directed attacks against the other in a geopolitical stratagem on the Peloponnese territory. Both sides had victories and losses. Athens was gaining significant inroads into the Peloponnese due to their successful naval raids and Sparta won several land battles invading Attica. In 454 BCE, Athens was forced to halt their aggression when their involvement to support an Egyptian revolt against the Persians ended in disaster, losing at least 40 ships from their naval fleet. Athens had been prosecuting a two-front war, which sufficiently distracted them from concentrating on either front, thus forcing them to seek a truce with Sparta. The armistice was brokered in 445 BCE between Sparta and Athens and was overconfidently called the Thirty Years Peace. It only lasted thirteen years because its purpose to achieve a lasting peace was undermined by Athens' actions.

Based on the settlement, Athens had given up its expanded territories on the Peloponnese; however, they continued to meddle with the affairs of the city-states in the Peloponnesian League, which incensed Sparta. In addition, Athens imposed economic sanctions on Megara, an ally of Sparta, preventing the city from trading in Athenian territory. Given Megara's proximity to Athenian territory, it had a disastrous impact on Megara; therefore Sparta declared war on Athens in 432 BCE.

Sparta renewed its invasion of Attica as it had done in the First Peloponnesian War. Athens' statesman and general, Pericles' (495 – 429 BCE) strategy at this time was to recall Athenians from the lands surrounding Athens into its fortified walls, knowing that the Peloponnesian League could only attack by land. Athens' port was securely protected and guaranteed Athens' ability to acquire supplies and conduct a naval war on the Peloponnesian League. Both sides conducted periodic, but ineffective incursions on the other's lands for several years. Athens' desire was to spur another helot uprising, while Sparta sought to demoralize the Athenians by burning their hinterland villages and farmlands. In an unfortunate turn of events for Athens, the city was beleaguered by the plague in 430 BCE and lost nearly a third of its citizens due to the tight living conditions resulting from Pericles' strategy. Also, Pericles himself perished in the blight, removing a key influence in Athens' leadership and self-confidence.

Despite this, both sides fought to a stalemate. Sparta's ability to field an army was dwindling after the many years of battle. It appeared as if Sparta would lose the struggle. With Pericles gone, Athens' leadership moved from his defensive strategy to an offensive one. Athens used Sparta's weakness as an opportunity to goad them into a major, open engagement which, given Athens' superior manpower, could potentially destroy Sparta's ability to make war for some time to come. This was a serious miscalculation. Athens overextended its military capabilities and in 418 BCE lost a decisive battle in Mantinea to the Spartans. This loss pushed the Athenians to devise a plan in 415 BCE, whereby they sailed a large expeditionary force to Sicily, west of Greece, in the hopes of strengthening Athens' presence in the Mediterranean. In a massive assault on Syracuse the Athenians were decimated, crippling Athens' naval and military capacities. The war would continue in various battles for the next fifteen years, ending with Athens - under siege, its treasury and supplies gone, city in ruins, military might nearly destroyed - capitulating to Sparta in 404 BCE.

5. Analysis & Conclusion

It appears that the strengths of Ancient Greece which developed over thousands of years turned out to be part of their undoing in the end. Athens, once the defender of Hellenic democracy, enlightenment, and reason, succumbed to the temptation of imperial power, greed and hegemony. Sparta, once Ancient Greece's staunch moral backbone gave way to arrogance, assuming itself to be the Hellenes' rightful leader, which in turn undermined democracy as they acted immorally. In an ironic fashion, the free Greeks acted out their tragedy in the manner of the great tragedians: Sophocles, Euripides and Aeschylus. The actions of the Spartans and Athenians resulted in extreme consequences; while used only as a device on the Greek stage, it manifested in the tragic realities of the Peloponnesian War. Greek killed fellow Greek, Persia regained much of its territories lost during the Persian Wars, and oligarchies and tyrants replaced democratic city-state assemblies. The war would ultimately weaken both Sparta and Athens, decimating their populations, leaving their lands destroyed and economies devastated. City-states no longer allied were often squabbling; their combined military forces were deteriorated, allowing foreign powers to infiltrate their homeland. These developments after the tragic war allowed the burgeoning Macedonian kingdom to fill the vacuum of power left by Athens and Sparta, affecting subsequent Greek generations.

Despite this, the city-states of Athens and Sparta continue to have a significant impact on modern civilization in various media, such as books, movies and TV. The fascination with this ancient civilization continues to be compelling to historians as well. Aside from the fact that these ancient city-states thrived and built some of the greatest artifacts in human history thousands of years ago, their ideas are what continue to arouse academic and popular curiosity, and for good reason.

The Ancient Greek *poleis*, while trading with one another, sharing a common heritage, belief system, geography and at times fighting enemies like the Persians as allies; had different customs and aspirations and periodically quarreled among themselves over territorial boundaries, trade and their *polis'* supremacy in the Ancient Greek world. Given this, and being the dominant Greek *poleis* in close proximity, much like in the Greek tragedies, Athens and Sparta were bound to clash. Due to Athens' and Sparta's significant reach and influences their clash would take on colossal proportions over decades which affected each *polis* and ultimately all of Ancient Greece for generations. This clash is known as the Peloponnesian War (431-404 BCE).

The customs, traditions and hegemony of both Athens and Sparta became factors for their similarities and differences as follows:

- Athens' ascendancy in Greece after the Greco-Persian Wars
- Sparta's evolution into a military state, becoming isolated and distrustful of rivals
- Athenian democracy vs. Spartan oligarchy
- Athens' and Sparta's distrust towards each other and holding of significant grievances between them.
- Leadership influences in Athens and Sparta
- Resulting effects of the Peloponnesian War

The Ancient Greeks had an aphorism inscribed on the Temple of Apollo at Delphi, stating, *"Gnothi seauton"* in Ancient Greek, meaning "know yourself". Based upon this, Socrates summarized and taught his students that the unexamined life is not worth living. From this, the Ancient Greeks - as in their famous comedies and tragedies - vacillated everywhere from tyranny to democracy. They had an honest contest of ideas. Like their artisans and craftsmen, Ancient Greece's philosophers, statesmen, generals and politicians created a dynamic society built upon lofty ideals. Their ideas fascinate and inspire Western Civilization to this day.

From the Ancient Greeks, parliamentary and representative democracies thrived through the ages. In this we can see more clearly the impact of Athens; however, we cannot disregard the fact that the extant record favors Athens. There is far much less historical material on Sparta. Given this, we cannot specifically say Athens is indeed the more influential city-state. But, as evidenced by what we do know, it appears very clear that the interchange and influence of both these city-states has endured through generations and continues to greatly impact Western Civilization.

Background

Historians, economists and political scientists can agree that ancient Greece was the first Western Civilization to significantly develop and expand Western concepts of democratic theory, economics and self-governance. Therefore, what were the conditions necessary in ancient Greece to create a fertile environment for such theories, culminating into their application in ancient Greek society?

Given that the Greek Archaic (750 - 500 BCE), Classical (500 to 336 BCE) and Hellenistic (336 - 146 BCE) periods combined have numerous contributions to Western culture, we will focus more on the two-hundred year period from the 5th Century BCE through the 4th Century BCE, referred to as Classical Greece, where many of today's notions of Greek philosophical and political thought are derived. Many other contributions were developed during this period in the disciplines of science, literature, art and architecture, but these will remain largely outside the scope of this analysis. Instead, we will concentrate on the conditions in ancient Greek society, mainly Athens, where the application of such developments occurred.

To illustrate what it meant to participate in Athenian society, Wijma notes that, "Many ancient sources…demonstrate that membership of the *polis* was not defined as a legal status with political privileges, but was rather conceived of as sharing or participating in the community, especially in the religious obligations of the *polis*."[1] One of the key insights in contrast to today's Western democracies is that community participation had greater emphasis than legal status. This will remain a core concept as we gain further insights into ancient Greek society. Additionally, the development of the *polis*[2], which means 'city' in Ancient Greek, was more about the concept of being an integral part of your city's activities or what modern interpretation calls 'citizenship'. (Today, the ancient Greek *polis* is often referred to as a 'city-state'). In fact, ancient Greeks were so connected to their respective *polis* that they

---

[1] Sara Wijma, *Joining the Athenian Community: the Participation of Metics in Athenian Polis Religion in the Fifth and Fourth Centuries B.C,* (Mnemosyne, 64, 3, 2011) 529 - 529.
[2] "polis", Dictionary.com. https://dictionary.reference.com/ (accessed August 12, 2012)

considered themselves citizens not of Greece, but Athenians or Spartans for example.

Modern use of the term democracy differs from the ancient Greek use in several ways, but the basic tenets follow the Greek word origin: in Greek, *demos*[3] translates to 'people' and *kratos*[4] translates to 'power' or 'people-power'. (Also, the Greek word *demokratia*[5] translates to 'popular government'.) So it's not surprising then that the *Declaration of Independence* begins with the words, "We the People", a very 'people-power' document that initialized a government, founded on the very same ancient Greek democratic principles that have endured for over 200 years in America, 100 years longer than the Athenian democratic government.

To understand the seminal environment in Ancient Greece that fostered free-thinking and experimentation, one must understand the diversity of Greek thought at that time. For example, *Michalides et al.* explains how such thought has impacted current concepts of Western economics (The word 'economics' comes from the Greek word *oikonomia* which literally translates to 'household management'[6]):

"The significant influence of ancient Greek thought on the writings of Classical economists is hard to be gainsaid. Adam Smith, for example, obtained considerable data from ancient Greek literature, not only in his major philosophical work, *The Theory of Moral Sentiments*, but also in his *Wealth of Nations*, the fundamental work of Classical Political Economy. Also, many economic problems have been treated in ancient Greek literature: for example, Aristotle's approach to the exchange process and private property, Xenophon's comments on the division of labour, as well as Plato's remarks on the same subject, are considered by

---

[3] "demos", Dictionary.com. https://dictionary.reference.com/ (accessed August 12, 2012)
[4] "kratos", Dictionary.com. http://dictionary.reference.com/ (accessed August 12, 2012)
[5] "demokratia", Dictionary.com. https://dictionary.reference.com/ (accessed August 12, 2012)
[6] "oikonomia", Dictionary.com. https://dictionary.reference.com/ (accessed August 12, 2012)

many authors to be some of the most famous ancient Greek contributions to economic thought."[7]

During the Classical Greek period, the diversity and volume of contributors to ancient Greek thought are profound. Given this, how do historians view the development and application of democratic concepts beginning with Greece and Athens? As referenced earlier, some historians assert that it was the need for military defense that caused democracy to begin. The Greek *polis* conscripted most of its male citizens as armed defenders called the 'hoplites'. Hoplites were citizen-soldiers. Vasillopulos states that, "...hoplites were a cause of the extension of full political participation for a major part of the Athenian citizenry...."[8] It seems that the impetus for citizens to rally and defend their city provided a significant opportunity to meet, speak of common concerns and work to address and resolve such issues once service was completed; but while fostering the right environment for democratic ideals, this was not the sole reason for their development. Vasillopulos further adds, "While the hoplite phalanx could not guarantee the development of democracy, neither could economic change no matter how pervasive, nor political philosophy no matter how profound."[9] Athenian society was built on the rule of law and a concept of equal rights for all citizens. Athens was the civic center of the Athenians' life. Citizens worked both in the city and throughout the countryside, farming or performing city labor. Athenians were united by their self-governance; they defended their city-state, supplied goods and worshiped the gods together as fundamental underpinnings of their society.

According to Swanson and Corbin, Aristotle, the well-known Athenian philosopher in his book *Politics* put forth that, "the city...like any living organism has a natural end, which [ends in] its most developed, mature and self-sufficient form. Political self-sufficiency is at

---

[7] Michaelides, Panayotis; Ourania Kardasi, John Milios, *Democritus's Economic Ideas in the Context of Classical Political Economy*, (European Journal of the History of Economic Thought, 18, 1, February 2011), 1-18.

[8] Christopher Vasillopulos, *The Nature of Athenian Hoplite Democracy*, (Armed Forces & Society, 22, 1, Fall 1995), 49-63.

[9] Ibid. Vasillopulos, 49-63.

least analogous to biological maturity."[10] Aristotle's view of natural law permeates the design of the Athenian city-state. His ideal governance is one whereby the citizens rule, or 'self-rule'. Aristotle expounds on the theme of the household as the initial building block of the ideal city state. He says the household must share private things publicly in order to be morally sound. A city-state is a union of many households. This action becomes his basis for a sound economy. Providing and sharing goods and services are fundamental to his economic principles. Citizen rule and the sharing household are critical to support the ideal city-state. He introduces other concepts like free speech so that citizens can debate what is good and bad for the household and city-state. Swanson and Corbin summarize by stating, "...by revealing nature's ends, he [Aristotle] charges human freedom with responsibility to those ends. We bear responsibility for the character of cities, and nature obliges us to make them good, just and self-sufficient by making us political or judgmental creatures."[11]

Aristotle treated several forms of governance in his book. One of the threats to democracy, however, was the return to the rule of the elite. Aristotle warned of the ills of despotism and aristocracy, but it was Athens' rejection of these forms of government that carved out its unique place in ancient history. This result, however, did not come without struggle. Deriving from its earliest clan beginnings, Athens emerged from its 'paternal' roots to form aristocracies based on wealth, land ownership and slavery, stemming from these first clans and their geographies. It was from these beginnings that Athenians toiled to emerge as a democratic city-state.

The *polis* (one Greek city-state) and the *poleis* (all Greek city-states) were dependent on one another. The *poleis* needed to build an economy that allowed for farming land, created goods, provided for ample trade and was secure against invasion. The Ancient Greeks celebrated their burgeoning growth by installing monuments and temples to the gods to express their gratitude. Cartlege says of it, "The *polis* was so successful an experiment that by the end of the Archaic period there were more

---

[10] ,Judith A. Swanson & David C. Corbin, *Aristotle's Politics*, (Continuum International Publishing, 2009), 179.
[11] Ibid. Swanson & Corben, 179.

21

Greek *poleis* sitting all around the Mediterranean and Black Sea shores."[12]

Gaeta asserts that the Athenian people's desire to distinguish themselves from then existing populations caused them to differentiate their internal spatial arrangements and control of their territorial proximity. He states:

"The great move of the Athenian people was the founding of political power in a spatial dimension, thus weakening (if not replacing) the relevance of bloodline relations and individual virtues. Athenians shaped their own space by drawing boundaries around their villages, the *demes*. Together with several units of people and places, providing the ground for the new constitutional framework, the first political space came into being. Such space does not belong to the power. It breeds power, and more precisely, a power system based on fundamental rights, irrespective of fortune or other birthrights."[13]

As discussed, this spatial control stemmed from strife within the Athenian city-state and the reforms that derived from several compromises between the disagreeing factions. These factions were loosely defined by their geographical and thus economic proximities. Athens had three primary regions: coastal, plains and mountainous territories. A significant imbalance occurred over time between these regions, threatening the unity of Athens. Consequently, radical changes needed to occur or Athens would face civil war.

One of the key leaders of reform was Solon, an early Athenian statesman and lawmaker. While not being credited with contemporary success, Solon's reforms formed the basis for a thriving democracy in Athens. Around 592 BCE, Solon instituted a series of changes. Gaeta explains, "The newly-appointed Solon effected reforms pivoted on a blanket extinction of debt together with the abrogation of enslavement for debtors, and the introduction of the system by which citizens were divided into census-classes in order to give more of the populace rightful access to public office and places in the army."[14] Unfortunately, Solon's

---

[12] Paul Cartledge, *The Birth of Greek Civilization*, (History Today, 33, 7, July 1983), 45.

[13] Luca Gaeta, *Athenian Democracy and the Political Foundation of Space*, (Planning Theory & Practice, 5, 4, December 2004), 471- 483.

[14] Ibid. Gaeta, 471- 483.

efforts were resisted, leading to ongoing and bitter struggles that would not let up for another generation. Despite this, Solon's efforts were recognized by political leaders as necessary means for common ground. Around 508 BCE, Cleisthenes, a noble and reformer of Athens, realized that Solon was correct in his observation that unless reform and equities were recreated in Athenian society, Athens would become weak, easily threatened by outside invaders, suffer from endless internal dissension and possibly slip into tyranny. Like Solon, Cleisthenes believed in participation by all ranks of society, to instill additional cohesion among the city-state. Fundamental to his reforms was dividing the three geographies into 30 equal territories with a balance of representation and power from each of the factions. Prior to Cleisthenes' changes, land was the sole property of heirs to aristocrats. It was his ingenious application of balancing power upon relative geographies that allowed for a radical, but sensible, transformation of Athenian political power. Gaeta summarizes that, "...the new equilibrium offered a different power-sharing system based on the distribution of inhabitants over the territory, and decisional power became the natural birthright of those born on the land of the *polis*."[15]

It is important to note that while ancient Athens emerged as an early form of democracy, its democratic principles of equality did not apply to everyone. Women, children and slaves did not share such rights. In fact, O'Neal explains, "In Athens, for the most part, women were legal nonentities whom the Greek male excluded any participation in the political or intellectual life of the city."[16] It seems their primary role was that of wife and mother, a role not undervalued by Athenians. Athenian literature, plays and art contained much about Greek women. Many classical works such as Homer's *Odyssey* contained females like Penelope as the archetypical wife. Or Xenophon's *Oeconomicus*, whereby he outlines the role of the wife in great detail, includes many domestic responsibilities. Remember, the Athenian household was the fundamental component of a proper functioning and morally sound city-state. A mother gives birth to and rears Athenian children, who are the

---

[15] Ibid. Gaeta, 471- 483.
[16] William J. O'Neal, *The Status of Women in Ancient Athens*, (International Social Science Review, 68, 3, Summer 1993), 115.

future of Athens' prosperity and security. Not an unimportant affair, but clearly not a participant in the public political life which now gets more negative attention. O'Neal summarizes that, "In this democracy, the city-state of almost 500,000 souls at its height had fewer than 15 percent of its people as citizens with equal and full rights."[17]

With regard to economics, according to Zenakis et al., "In addition to the arts and philosophy the Ancient Greeks contributed greatly to the ideas and practices of economic and social decision making."[18] They attribute to Xenophon the first concepts of economic and scientific management, where practices of such played out within the Athenian city-state. Xenophon was a writer and historian, living from 430-355 BCE. He wrote several books on economics, of which his *Oeconomicus* was chief among them. He is attributed with the treating of goods production, monetary savings, an equitable sharing of wealth and a commerce-based economy. Xenophon calls for a hard-work ethic built upon a knowledgeable steward of the business in which they are responsible. He introduced the first concepts of supply and demand when he looked at the shortage of gold supply which increased its value. He put forward early concepts of business management and bond market financing, which at that time was simply a group of citizens contributing private money to fund business enterprises and received interest in return.

According to Zenakis et al., "Even though many of Xenophon's ideas were not adopted or implemented, money lending and savings practices increased significantly during his time, supporting Pericles' Golden Age and the prosperity of the Athenian democracy."[19]

In the face of such success, Athenians still believed in the just state and that wealth was not an end unto itself, but should serve the greater good and have moral purpose. Democritus (460 – 370 BCE), an early Greek philosopher and scientist noted for his ethical contributions to Greek thought, was a proponent of democracy but disdained

---

[17] William J. O'Neal, *The Status of Women in Ancient Athens*, (International Social Science Review, 68, 3, Summer 1993), 115.

[18] Stelios Zanakis, Stavros Theofanides, Anthony Kontaratos, Theodosios Tassios, *Ancient Greeks' Practices and Contributions in Public and Entrepreneurship Decision Making* (Interfaces 33, 6, Nov/Dec 2003), 72-88.

[19] Ibid. Zanakis et al., 72-88.

overconsumption. He believed that economic dealings should be based upon justice. Michalides, et al. makes clear, "Democritus insisted on the superiority of spiritual, moral and psychological pleasures as opposed to material ones."[20]

It is Democritus that is credited for initial thoughts on the division of labor being a significant contributor to successful productivity and the remote foundation of industrialization. Such a cooperation of labor forces is a connected and interdependent labor force that maximizes output while conserving resources. Much of modern economics is built upon this principle. Many historians, philosophers and economists such as Plato, Xenophon, David Hume and Adam Smith have shared his opinion in this regard.

While ancient Greek thought regarding economics remained primarily theoretical, it is difficult to argue that their contributions did not fuel economic practices in many societies thereafter. Michalides, et al. summarizes Democritus' contributions well:

"The central point of the Democritian philosophy seems to be the prevalence of logic and justice over society... all social issues, including political and economic relationships, become essentially ethical issues. Moreover, we can identify a much more particular epistemological influence of ancient Greek, and more specifically of the Democritian philosophy, on Classical Political Economy: namely the conception that (economic) phenomena possess an inherent, law-determined causality and regularity (a concept also shared by the natural sciences)...."[21]

While it is ubiquitous and clear that Western civilization is deeply grounded in early Greek thought, the Ancient Greeks themselves were fully aware of the challenges to their ideals. We should not take from this review a false image of perfection stemming from Ancient Greek society. The Greek *poleis* were often controlled by selfish, power-seeking aristocrats and even 'tyrants' as they called despotic leaders. The word tyrant comes from the Greek *tyrannos*. Such tyrants often usurped political power in the *poleis* whether by aggression or political clout. Consequently, the populace would be forced to recapture its own self-

---

[20] Panayotis Michaelides, Ourania Kardasi, John Milios, *Democritus's Economic Ideas in the Context of Classical Political Economy*, (European Journal of the History of Economic Thought, 18, 1, February 2011), 1-18.
[21] Ibid. Michaelidies et al., 1-18.

governance from such leaders. This occurred several times throughout the Ancient Greek period. The word 'demagogue' was also invented by the Ancient Greeks describing those who seize power and exploit the populace's lack of understanding of political issues, appealing to their strong passions and thus arousing sensational actions. According to Lane, "The Athenians did have variegated concepts of bad political leadership, and they did have the idea of a form of political leadership appealing particularly to the common people as opposed to the elite."[22] Despite these challenges, Athenians strove to have good, strong leadership as opposed to tyrants or demagogues. Athenians understood that men were required to be assertive and vocal in the public assembly, or in court, to ensure democratic ideals were fought for and represented well. Thus, the opposite of tyrants and demagogues were statesmen. Lane also notes that many early Greek historians and philosophers compared and contrasted behavior of specific leaders as being demagogues or statesmen. She explains, "Surely, we think, the statesman-demagogue distinction is as central to Aristophanes as it is to Thucydides."[23] Their works are discussed and were critical of the actions of Athenian leaders like Cleon (considered a statesman) and Cleophon (considered a demagogue), both during the Peloponnesian War. This is how political life was treated in Athenian society.

Many Greek and other subsequent historians reveal that it was a series of unique environmental, political, military and societal conditions that made it possible for Ancient Greece to develop Western democratic thought, free-market economics and political self-governance. While these conditions are present in most civilizations, it was Ancient Greece's, and more specifically Ancient Athens' people that made a difference. If all of life's processes and changes stem from the human mind and heart, it was Ancient Greece's ability to communicate and experiment with theories of political, economic and spiritual life that provided for a dynamic atmosphere of growth. Ancient Greece had no shortage of thinkers, statesmen, politicians, generals, artisans, artists, playwrights, architects and so on. Some good, some bad, but in a general

---

[22] Melissa Lane, *The Origins of the Statesman--Demagogue Distinction in and after Ancient Athens* (Journal of the History of Ideas, 73, 2, April 2012), 179-200.
[23] Ibid. Lane, 179-200.

milieu of freedom, all of these contributed to an astounding corpus of human knowledge and creativity. Such knowledge and creativity would affect and inspire subsequent civilizations such as the Roman and Arabic cultures and extend into early European society and modern Western civilizations.

However, before we assign premature conclusions to this rudimentary research, we must acknowledge that Ancient Greek democracy, economics and thought were not perfected. Additionally, we cannot correlate such concepts directly to modern forms of democracy. Many of the concepts they employed embodied multiple forms of government and economics which today could be interpreted as 'socialist' or 'communist' (which take on very different meanings today); while in other instances they were 'capitalists' and 'republicans'. Certainly, it was the ideal that human beings are at their best when they are free which has triumphed in certain times and societies throughout the ages. The concepts of natural law, human rights, equality, fair representation and ultimately the freedom of humanity were vital steps for the progress of Western society. It was these notions that inspired the *Magna Carta,* Humanism in the Middle Ages, the English Glorious Revolution of 1688 and The Declaration of Independence. Human freedom has faced down tyranny and opened the human spirit to unprecedented creativity. It appears that historians agree that the founders of such inspiration were indeed the ancient Greeks.

Chapter I - Works Cited

1. Wijma, Sara. *Joining the Athenian Community: The Participation of Metics in Athenian Polis Religion in the Fifth and Fourth Centuries BC.* Mnemosyne: Vol. 64, 3, (2011). 529-529.

2. Michaelides, Panayotis, Ourania Kardasi, and John Milios. *Democritus's Economic Ideas in the Context of Classical Political Economy.* European Journal of the History of Economic Thought: 18, 1, (February 2011). 1-18.

3. Vasillopulos, Christopher. *The Nature of Athenian Hoplite Democracy.* Armed Forces & Society: 22, 1, (Fall 1995). 49-63.

4. Swanson, Judith A., and David C. Corbin. *Aristotle's Politics.* Continuum International Publishing: 2009. 179.

5. Cartledge, Paul. *The Birth of Greek Civilization.* History Today: 33, 7, (July 1983). 45.

6. Gaeta, Luca. *Athenian Democracy and the Political Foundation of Space.* Planning Theory & Practice: 5, 4, (December 2004). 471-483.

7. O'Neal, William J. *The Status of Women in Ancient Athens.* International Social Science Review: 68, 3, (Summer 93). 115.

8. Zanakis, Stelios, Stavros Theofanides, Anthony Kontaratos, and Theodosios Tassios. *Ancient Greeks' Practices and Contributions in Public and Entrepreneurship Decision Making.* Interfaces: 33, 6, (November/December 2003). 72-88.

9. Lane, Melissa. *The Origins of the Statesman--Demagogue Distinction in and after Ancient Athens.* Journal of the History of Ideas: 73, 2, (April 2012(. 179-200.

Chapter I - Works Consulted

Anastasiadis, V.I. *Idealized ΣΧΟΛΗ and Disdain for Work: Aspects of Philosophy and Politics in Ancient Democracy*. Classical Quarterly, 54, 1 (2004): 58-79.

Anderson, Greg. *The Personality of the Greek State*. Journal of Hellenic Studies, 129 (2009): 1-22.

Arnason, Johann P. *Castoriadis as a Civilizational Analyst: Sense and Nonsense in Ancient Greece*. European Journal of Social Theory, 15, 3 (August 2012): 295-311.

Balot, Ryan. *Courage in the Democratic Polis*. Classical Quarterly, 54, 2 (2004): 406-423.

Bosnak, Azize. *Inquiring Into the Origins of Ancient Greece and the Aryan Model in Blackathena by Martin Bernal*. Journal of Academic Studies, 13, 50 (August-October 2011): 65-74.

Cartledge, Paul. *The Birth of Greek Civilization*. History Today, 33, 7, (July 1983): 45.

de Benoist, Alain. *Democracy Revisited*. Telos, 95, (Spring 1993): 65.

Elden, Stuart. *Another Sense of Demos: Kleisthenes and the Greek Division of the Polis*. Democratization, 10, 1 (Spring 2003): 135-156.

Fleck, Robert K., and Andrew F. Hanssen. *The Origins of Democracy: A Model with Application to Ancient Greece*. Journal of Law & Economics, 49, 1, (April 2006): 115-146.

Gaeta, Luca. *Athenian Democracy and the Political Foundation of Space*. Planning Theory & Practice, 5, 4, (December 2004): 471-483.

Lane, Melissa. *The Origins of the Statesman--Demagogue Distinction in and after Ancient Athens*. Journal of the History of Ideas, 73, 2 (April 2012): 179-200.

Michaelides, Panayotis, Ourania Kardasi, and John Milios. *Democritus's Economic Ideas in the Context of Classical Political Economy*. European Journal of the History of Economic Thought, 18, 1 (February 2011): 1-18.

Ober, Josiah. *What the Ancient Greeks Can Tell Us About Democracy*. Annual Review of Political Science, 11, 1 (2008): 67-91.

O'Neal, William J. *The Status of Women in Ancient Athens*. International Social Science Review, 68, 3 (Summer 1993): 115.

Russett, Bruce, and William Antholis. *Do Democracies Fight Each Other? Evidence from the Peloponnesian War*. Journal of Peace Research, 29, 4 (November 1992): 415.

Stoll, Oliver. *For the Glory of Athens: Xenophon's Hipparchikos <Logos>, A TechnicalTtreatise and Instruction Manual on Ideal Leadership*. Studies in History & Philosophy of Science, Part A, 43, 2 (June 2012): 250-257.

Strauss, Barry. *American Democracy Through Ancient Greek Eyes*. History Today, 44, 4, (April 1994): 32, 292.

Swanson, Judith A., and David C. Corbin. *Aristotle's Politics*. Continuum International Publishing: 2009. 179.

Toth, Imre. *Antiquity, Modernity and the Permanence of Relationship*. Museum International, 62, 3, (September 2010): 6-8.

Westgate, Ruth. *The Greek House and the Ideology of Citizenship*. World Archaeology, 39, 2, (June 2007): 229-245.

Wijma, Sara. *Joining the Athenian Community: The Participation of Metics in Athenian Polis Religion in the Fifth and Fourth Centuries B.C.* Mnemosyne, 64, 3, (2011): 529-529.

"*Back to the Polis*." Economist, 332, 7881 (9/17/1994): 63-64.

"*The Costs of Freedom*." Chronicle of Higher Education, 51, 46 (7/22/2005): B4.

Vasillopulos, Christopher. *The Nature of Athenian Hoplite Democracy*. Armed Forces & Society, 22, 1, (Fall 1995): 49-63.

Zanakis, Stelios, Stavros Theofanides, Anthony Kontaratos, and Theodosios Tassios. "*Ancient Greeks' Practices and Contributions in Public and Entrepreneurship Decision Making*." Interfaces, 33, 6, (Nov/Dec 2003): 72-88.

Zatta, Claudia. *Conflict, People, and City-Space: Some Exempla from Thucydides' History*. Classical Antiquity, 30, 2, (October 2011): 318-350.

Chapter II

Ancient Roman Law: From *Mos Maiorum* and Early Civil Law to the Constitution of the Roman Republic, the Law of the Twelve Tables, and the Early Formation of the Roman Legal System

Historiography

Introduction

Rome, a small, obscure agricultural village grew to become one of the greatest political and military empires of the ancient world. There are several factors and cultural characteristics that contributed to Rome's successes in the creation of a Republic, later an empire and ultimately its decline. Its cultural foundation was based on the work, interaction and agreements between the plebeians (general population) and the patricians (oligarchs). Through a modern lens, it is generally true that the patricians were the wealthy and the plebeians were less so, but often patricians lost their fortunes and plebeians became wealthy. The titles of patrician and plebeian were more appropriately titles by birthright, so wealth had less to do with the title than social status.

1. Roman Historians

The Romans viewed their own history as unique, departing from the Ancient Greeks' mainly because the Romans could point back to the *Annals Maximi*, a recording of historical events, participants and outcomes begun during the Roman Republic. Rome's earliest historians such as Cato the Elder (234-149 BCE) began using Latin instead of Greek as in his monograph *Origines* which relayed Rome's history from its founding to Cato's present day. Quintus Fabius Pictor (circa. 270 BCE) is recognized as the founder of Rome's particular style of historiography. His accounts are considered very favorable to Rome and he places Rome's founding at 747 BCE. Early Roman historians were pragmatic and intended to present objective facts and balanced interpretations. More modern historians argue that Roman historians wrote favorably of Rome's way of life, its morals and its government.

Notable modern historians include England's Edward Gibbon (1737 – 1794 CE), who wrote *The History of the Decline and Fall of the Roman Empire*. Gibbon's thesis claims that Rome's acceptance of Christianity was a catalyst for its decline. Gibbon's work prevailed as the definitive interpretation until modern historians such as Germany's

Theodor Mommsen (1817 – 1903 CE) began to question Gibbon's thesis. Mommsen analyzed Rome by placing its key foundations in modern historical context as a nation-state, including democratic and imperial principles. Mommsen's works remain relevant to modern historians. A.H.M. Jones of England (1904-1970 CE) is noted for his work on the later Roman Empire which until his time was largely understudied.

2. Ancient Origin

Rome's founding begins in the remote past. Much of Rome's beginnings are rooted in the ancient religious practices of the Etruscans and their *Mos Maiorum* (The ancient traditions and practices of the Roman tribes). Early Roman culture was also imported from Ancient Greece. The Italian peninsula's southern and coastal regions were called *Magna Graecia* (greater Greece). Patricians were the ruling class of families. The plebeians were the group of free Roman citizens. Together, these two groups who were often in conflict developed the burgeoning Roman Republic. Rome's early leadership, from approximately 510 BCE, was under a series of kings (rex). The Roman kings led the local populace in battle, religious ceremonies and cultural traditions. It was under these actions that local tribes and villages (who filled the plebeian class) drew together under Roman auspices, making Rome a larger community. The kings were family leaders drawn from the patrician class. In the pecking order of Roman society, the aristocracy came after the king. Aristocrats played a significant leadership role in their formation of the council of elders called the senate. They also had a lock on religious roles such as high priests. Such aristocratic families would hold their positions for generations and would later become the patricians of Republican Rome and later the Roman Empire.

These family clans (*gentes*) formed the basis for Roman society. Since Rome's military was a citizen army, the *gentes* (land-owners) were required to supply men-at-arms for civil defense. This structure would change over the centuries as demand for manpower increased.

34

3. Republic to Empire

Ancient Rome was a society made up of tribes living on the Italian peninsula at that time. In time, the various tribes figured out ways to settle differences and develop a highly functioning culture. Rome included peoples from Latium and the mysterious Etruscans (Etruria) who previously dominated its culture from the 7th to the 5th centuries BCE. The Etruscans handed down the ancient Roman religion and monarchy (*Regum Romanum*). Etruscan control eventually yielded to an oligarchical class known as the patricians.

The patricians did away with the monarchy and developed a republican government under a council of elders (senate). The senate would dominate Roman leadership for several centuries under the Roman Republic. Rome's rivals and challenges under these structures would enhance its survival. The senate would prosecute conflicts, wars and tribal actions that integrated the best of its rivals' military prowess, social norms, religions and cultures. The Italic tribes over time would fold into the Roman Republic or be vanquished. Ancient Rome didn't accept the close proximity of competitors. Once Rome had consolidated its political, economic, social and religious structures, it would proceed to both challenge and defend itself in the ancient Mediterranean world. Due to the coordinated efforts of its political, economic and military power (*imperium*), Rome would advance to conquer or make as vassals the ancient Mediterranean peoples.

Early in the Roman Republic prior to 300 BCE, five revolts called the Conflict of the Orders caused the patricians to relinquish power and establish plebeian offices previously blocked to plebeians: tribunes of the people (military or political leaders) and *aediles* (public office holders). It was also at this time that the Law of the Twelve Tables gave the right of plebeian/patrician intermarriage which would change the prior social order significantly. High government offices and priesthoods were also opened to the plebeians.

Ancient Rome was also a product of the Ancient Greek and Hellenistic civilizations. The influences of Greek philosophy, literature, military and especially government were profound. Greek civilization, through its maritime activity, was present on the ancient Italian peninsula during Rome's ascendancy and would also be absorbed into Roman culture. Such influences are readily seen in ancient Rome's architecture, religions and eventually its intellectual expression. It is noted that Rome's first authors wrote in Greek and saw themselves as an offshoot of the Greek civilization. In fact, much of the early Roman territory on the southern Italian peninsula is referred to as *Magna Graecia* (Greater Greece). This would eventually give way to a series of Roman intellectuals, political leaders and philosophers who saw Rome as its own unique and distinct civilization.

Rome's ascendancy from its humble roots through its grand Republic would culminate in the power and tyranny of the Roman Empire. It is through these developments that Rome's cultural nature was tested. While it remains one of history's longest lasting world superpowers, it would ultimately fall, leaving a vacuum in place of the more advanced civilization Rome created in its wake and for the Western peoples to rebuild its former glories. In the East, the Byzantine Civilization (Eastern Roman Empire) picked up where the Western Roman Empire receded.

Roman society's foundations were enshrined within its values and morals, encoded into its elaborate legal system, and memorialized through its traditions and practices known as the *mos maiorum* that was handed down from previous generations. Ancient Rome was not only an historical place and civilization, but a deeply moral or principled culture steeped in religion and based upon a solid foundation of social customs and traditions. In its seminal period, before Rome established itself as a firm polity, these social customs were unwritten, but deeply rooted in their tribal norms, mores and folkways. Like the Ancient Greeks, the Romans believed that piety to the gods as a standard practice was utterly essential in order to maintain their vitality and hegemony. The honoring, memorializing and observation of these cultural, religious, social and moral standards are what made Ancient Rome a strong and vibrant civilization. Their laws and traditions guided their decision-making processes and they showed a dynamic ability to adapt and assimilate their culture to challenges and adversities.

As previously indicated, Ancient Rome was also subject to the conflicts and changes it endured throughout its history. As the Republic fell due to its internal strife and failures of leadership, other leaders, deeply ingrained with the Roman *mos maiorum*, like Augustus, reformed the imperiled Republic. Ancient Rome which survived under the Republic from approximately 500 BCE to 27 BCE was revived under Augustus' reforms. The *Pax Romana* (Roman Peace) that he initiated would prevail for another 200 years until what historians point to as its ending around the death of Marcus Aurelius in 180 CE. These years are marked as the *Principate*, where the role of "first citizen" (or what is now viewed as the emperor) had major control of the Roman government and military affairs.

Rome evolved from a Republic consisting of the Roman Senate and Consul (where the wealthy ruling class of elders or *Patricians* ruled through consensus and conciliation) to Empire, where the Senate did more routine tasks of government and the Emperor acted as an authoritarian. The plebeians were a social class that did not hold familial title as did the patricians, but after the Conflict of the Orders they acquired political power as a counterweight to the influence of the patricians. The status of both classes changed and migrated as Rome evolved from Republic to Empire.

4. Long Road to Decline

Rome ruled much of the Mediterranean from its beginning as the Roman Republic in 500 BCE to its height under Augustus Caesar in the 1st century BCE. The Empire endured a tumultuous decline until its collapse in the West around 500 CE. There are many reasons for its decline. Rome's beliefs shifted from the *mos maiorum* to Christianity, there was a steady influx of barbarian tribes who diluted Roman order, and they were unable to manage its monetary policy that led to recession and collapse. All classes of Roman society were affected by its decline. By the Late Roman Empire, the title of patrician had lost most of its meaning and sway within Roman society.

For 300 years after Marcus Aurelius, the Roman Empire would endure and at times self-inflict seismic changes to its cultural, moral, military, social, governmental and economic profile. Christianity gained significant ground as a sub-cultural movement that was fueled by the

Empire's efforts to suppress its influences. Christianity had multiple effects on Roman culture; mainly it would replace classical Roman thought, religion and philosophy and become a conduit that carried its beliefs beyond the Roman borders, which had the result of diluting major underpinnings of Roman civilization and creating unity among Romans and barbarian cultures against Ancient Rome. After the Crisis of the third century (235-284 CE), where the Roman Empire heaved under pressures from barbarian invasions, economic failure and internal conflict, Diocletian (emperor, 245-311 CE) through military and governmental successes instituted reforms halting the crisis, but splintered the Empire into four sovereign geographies. While this would preserve the Empire for a period, the consequences of the split would begin a new era of challenges where the Eastern and Western provinces would, in time, form an insurmountable divide. Without more significant adjustments to the factors that were leading to the Empire's decline, Diocletian's reforms were only temporary measures.

After this period, historians point to several defining circumstances leading to the decline of the classical Roman civilization. The Western Empire was overcome by the barbarian invasions and the strength of the Germanic tribes who resisted Rome's influence. The rise of the *Germani* and their organizational structures peaked as Western Rome's power waned; its economy petered out and its civilization was disorganized. This decaying infrastructure was compounded by governmental and economic policies that acted as a catalyst for its decline. The gap between rich and poor and an unequal distribution of taxes on rural citizens over urban citizens bankrupted the West. Also, there evolved over time the deterioration of the ancient social/religious practices of Rome which was replaced with Christianity. These practices were the lifeblood of ancient Rome and Christianity was a new influence which was pervasive throughout the ancient world; no longer distinguishing Rome as a distinct culture.

Romanitas (The Roman Way) was replaced by the influx of disparate cultures impacting the Roman civic sense of duty and loyalty to the *mos maiorum* of Rome. This had the outcome of adulterating the integrity of the Roman army, which weakened against the increased onslaught of barbarian invasions. As Romans moved away from their classical roots, their cohesiveness and adherence to such driving and rallying principles faded, leaving the Roman Empire susceptible to disintegration. This also manifested in the actions of various emperors after Marcus Aurelius. The continued civil strife, assassinations, pretenders and competitors to the post of emperor led to moral and leadership failure. The government was often at the mercy of military coups and despotic leaders.

The economy of Rome was not sophisticated enough to endure the radical changes that occurred after the Crisis of the Third Century. It appears that populations in the West declined, tribute from conquest all but disappeared and the overbearing tax system caused widespread poverty. Without financial stability and poor currency valuation, local territories receded from Rome's support and the economic infrastructure collapsed. Urban populations abandoned cities and migrated to lands that could provide basic survival through farming. In the wake of such changes, trade and industry also collapsed which was an additional strike against the Roman economy. Citizens, under the belief that by abandoning the cities they could hide from onerous governmental laws, sought freedom in the countryside in what became estates turned fortresses. These fortresses initiated what became the feudal system of the medieval period. Citizens relied on the protection and economies of these fortresses as the Empire's ability to protect its people and manage day-to-day affairs failed.

There is also evidence that as contact with the Middle East increased through wars and trade, disease followed. Roman lifestyle, through the use of public facilities, increased the spread of pathogens, whereas barbarian infrastructure maintained more isolated living, thus decreasing barbarian epidemics while Rome's increased simultaneously. These actions appeared to Christians as God's wrath on the Romans for their mistreatment at the hands of the Romans, further bolstering the view that Rome was decadent and deserved its demise. The rise of Middle Eastern powers also coincided with the attacks in the West, and like so many failed armies throughout history, fighting two-front wars wreaked havoc on the Empire's resources, further destabilizing and debilitating its military and economic footing.

Both patricians and plebeians suffered similar fates by the end of the Western Roman Empire. Titles were relatively meaningless and those left with land and wealth were forced to retreat into the countryside and entrench themselves behind fortifications to maintain their economy, order and protection from the chaos that followed Rome's decline.

5. Conclusion

No one event caused Rome to fall. There were many complex issues that caused it to decline. One can conclude that it did not fall but evolved into what is now recognized as Western civilization. In the early Roman Empire, patrician status still had some prestige. Roman emperors often elevated their supporters to patricians; however, by the 3rd century and through the decline of the Western Roman Empire, all meaning and prestige of the patrician status was degraded and no longer resembled anything of what it was under the Roman Republic. Constantine the Great restored the title of patrician as an honorific title and limited it to a very small number where it remained a high title in the Byzantine Empire.

Background

The ancient Roman legal system was developed over many years beginning with Etruscan religious practices. It continued to evolve through the early Roman monarchy, the establishment of the patricians and the political struggle between the plebeians and the Roman social hierarchy. We will examine the developmental stages of the ancient Roman legal system and how it progressed through the establishment of the *Law of the Twelve Tables* and the *Constitution of the Roman Republic*.

As discussed, Ancient Rome was not only an historical place and civilization, but a deeply moral or principled culture steeped in religion and based upon a solid foundation of social customs and traditions. In its seminal period, before Rome established itself as a firm polity, these social customs were unwritten, but deeply rooted in their tribal norms, mores and folkways. These customs are known in Latin as the *mos maiorum* or ancestral customs, literally "custom (way) of our ancestors (elders)." Although unwritten, the *mos maiorum* provided the moral inspiration that propelled disparate tribes to gather and flourish into one of the greatest civilizations of the ancient world and one that would also shape future societies.

Like many ancient societies, the family (or *gens*) was the core of ancient Roman society. The *gens* were family that shared the same *nomen* (family clan name) and descended from the same ancestor. Roman society was patriarchal and the *paterfamilias* (oldest male with the *gens nomen*) was the head of the *familia* (family). The *mos maiorum* required that the *paterfamilias* acted with a high degree of integrity and it applied social pressure on him to follow the ancient customs and to exhibit deeply-ingrained values which included, but were not limited to: respect (for the family and other families), personal credibility by being straightforward and reliable (especially in the military), virtue (pursuing right behavior as defined by Roman society), religious piety (honoring the gods and observing religious practices), and discipline (as a soldier, student and contributor to Roman society).

While the *familia* was an autonomous social unit, the Romans saw it as important and necessary to reinforce such values by incorporating their oversight into its political institutions. Consequently, the office of *censor* was designated, in addition to conducting the census, to police the public morality *(regimen morum)*. The *censor* was an executive magistrate that served the Roman Republic and who previously held the office of *consul*. The *consuls* were the highest elected officials from the senate and led the government of the Roman Republic. *Consuls* and *censors* were initially taken from the patrician class exclusively, thus revealing how important the Roman's viewed this office's function. The *comitia centuriata* was the only leadership body in the Roman Republic that could elect a *consul* or *censor*. Under the *Constitution of the Roman Republic*, the *comitia centuriata* was comprised of citizen-soldiers based on property ownership and total wealth. This body was wholly aristocratic and dominated by the patricians.

The *censor* presided over the public and private affairs of Roman citizens and enforced the *mos maiorum* and the *regimen morum*. Their duties included, but were not limited to: oversights of marital matters, procreation, marital divorce, domestic violence, lifestyle activity, household maintenance, slave management, public behavior, military conduct, legal decorum, and so on. The *censors* had judicial power to brand citizens so that their public and private ranking could be reduced. Such power supported the *censors'* authority. They also had access to punishments that could be imposed, which included barring citizens from public office or banishment from one's tribe. Subsequent *censors*, however, could reverse a branded citizen's status. As such, c*ensors* were given significant power to enforce the *regimen morum*. The fact that the Romans made this role an executive magistrate (second only to the *consuls*) emphasizes the importance they placed on public and private behavior and their desire to perpetuate Roman traditions.

Looking back at earlier cultural developments prior to 500 BCE (750 BCE to 500 BCE), the Romans derived much of their identity from the combination of their Latin tribal beginnings and their comingling with the Etruscan civilization. The Etruscans provided Roman culture with concepts of societal order. We can attribute to this period the uniting of loosely affiliated tribes located in the vicinity of Rome. This unity provided for the establishment of the 'city' as we now recognize it. With unity came greater organization and the application of group projects in engineering, architecture and public infrastructure projects. According to Cary and Scullard, "The Etruscans perhaps provided the stimulus which provoked the scattered villagers to greater unity; they certainly provided the architectural and engineering skill which produced the new buildings of the city of Rome."[24] The Etruscans, while still somewhat hidden by the lack of written history, limited archaeological findings and extant artifacts, are attributed with much of Rome's cultural roots in architecture, art, sculpture, pottery decoration, defensive earthworks, economic productivity (mainly agricultural), family organization, religion, social and political structures, military formation and government which was a combination of monarchy (*rex* or kings) under the Roman Kingdom and the formation of the senate (*senatus consulta*); essentially most aspects of Roman life. After 500 BCE, Etruscan dominance would be replaced by a uniquely Roman culture that culminated through years of development under the Etruscan monarchy. The *senate* (elders) would move from a consultative body under the Roman Kingdom to one of leadership, replacing the Etruscan *rex* as the supreme governing authority of Rome in conjunction with the ruling assemblies of the people. These changes formed the Roman Republic.

The Roman Republic was grounded in the maturation and transformation of Roman society under the Roman Kingdom. The formation of the Republic was not a stark or speedy transition, but was the amalgam of political, economic, social and governmental modifications over time that led to revolution. The patricians (*patricius*) who were the landed aristocracy of Rome constituted the ruling class. The patricians occupied the senate and the executive magistracies. It was the acquisition of wealth, power and prestige among the patricians that caused the monarchy to be replaced. There was too much opportunity among too many men of equal status to answer to one authority. The patricians, however, respected central authority and retained the workings of the senate - after the deposition of the *rex* - but it became more of a deliberative body, making recommendations to the magistrates

---

[24] M. Cary and H.H. Scullard. *A History of Rome* (New York: Palgrave Publishers, 1975), 42.

which were followed nearly all the time. The senate's recommendations were acted upon and led by the *consuls*, who directed government and military activities. The Roman Republic had an intricate governmental system of checks and balances and a separation of powers in direct reaction to the previous monarchical structure. Le Glay, Voisin and Le Bohec observe:

"...it is possible to follow the birth of the Republic, marked chiefly by the institution of the consulship and the first battles against the people of Latium. The period is characterized by internal struggles within the Roman state, as well as by conflict with its neighbors. Thus, between 450 BC and 390 BC Rome was seeking a balance in both areas. This balance was reached by the organization of its political institutions and by the formation of a new body of 'nobles.'"[25]

While the patricians were the wealthy elite of the Roman Kingdom and early Roman Republic, they were only a small subset of the Roman population. Making up the remainder were the wealthier working classes and poor known as the Plebeians (*plebeius*). The periodic census determined who was a patrician and who was a plebeian. Plebeians included small property owners, artisans, laborers, peddlers and shopkeepers, and skilled and unskilled workers. In the years immediately following the removal of the monarchy, Rome would wrangle with the establishment of its government and the working relationship between the patricians and plebeians. This is now known as the "struggle of the orders." This struggle was based in the plebeians' want of appropriate representation in government as a counter to patrician dominance of high government positions and general control of Roman society. The patricians began to cede some powers to the plebeians and consequently "Tribunes of the People" (*tribuni plebis*) were appointed to represent their interests. In recognition of the pressures from new populations entering Roman culture (after successful conquest) and the need for greater representation of the plebeians, the patricians temporarily dissolved the *consuls* and replaced them with an extraordinary legislative body that exercised emergency powers to address the urgency of this conflict. This body was called the *decemvirate* (ten men). They were

---

[25] Marcel LeGlay, Jean-Louis Voisin, and Yann Le Bohec, *A History of Rome* (West Sussex: Wiley-Blackwell, 2009), 43.

selected from the patricians and plebeians and empowered with *consular imperium* (sovereign authority) to adjudicate solutions to the political upheaval. Livy (Titus Livius Patavinus 59 BCE -17 CE), in his history of Rome, attributed the founding of Roman law to the *decemvirate*. Le Glay, et. al. continue that, "The task of the legislators was to ensure that the law would be equal for all citizens."[26] In 451 BCE, after two years of deliberation, the *decemvirate* produced the *Twelve Tables of Roman Law* replacing the oral traditions of Roman law.

Prior to discussing the Twelve Tables, it is helpful to take a step back and see how the Roman Republic's government worked. As previously discussed, the Republic was built on an unwritten moral code known as the *mos maiorum*. This moral code was enacted into the *Constitution of the Roman Republic*. The *Constitution of the Roman Republic* made it possible for the selection of the *decemvirate*. The *decemvirate* then produced the Law of the Twelve Tables. The *Constitution of the Roman Republic* was organized as follows:

- The *Comitia Centuriata* was the assembly of citizen-soldiers that required total wealth as a prerequisite for entrance. This was an aristocratic body and responsible for the election of higher magistrates: *consuls, praetors and censors.*
- The *Senate* was made up of members from the *comitia centuriata* who had previous military and/or governmental experience. The senate directed all government affairs at home and abroad. The senate issued orders to the magistrates.
- The *Comitia Tributa* was the tribal council whereby each tribe of Rome was afforded voting rights. Patricians and plebeians were part of this assembly. While this group had wealthier classes it was a mixture of lower wealth classes and plebeians. This body was responsible for the election of lower level magistrates: *quaestors* (financial managers), and *curule aediles*(responsible for temple and infrastructure building).
- *Consilium Plebis* was comprised only of plebeians and presided over by a tribune of the people. This body elected tribune

---

[26] Marcel LeGlay, Jean-Louis Voisin, and Yann Le Bohec, *A History of Rome* (West Sussex: Wiley-Blackwell, 2009), 47.

45

magistrates: plebeian tribune and plebeian *aedile*. Tribunes had veto power with all governmental assemblies.

This system of government was designed to provide checks and balances, separation of power and a balance of power. It was not always successful; therefore, around 450 BCE, due to the strident demands of the plebeians and their threat of secession from Rome, it required the interdiction of the *decemvirate* to provide a codification of Rome's legal structure providing for additional balance of power and equality for all Roman citizens.

In response to these developments, the government halted its ordinary functions in dealing with internal challenges, suspended the offices of *consul* and the other magistracies, while the patricians and plebeians commissioned ten men, granting them *imperium* and extraordinary powers to address and resolve the impasse between the orders. The *decemvirate* consulted the Athenian constitutional framework and the Greek lawgivers of the *Areopagus*, having experience from the reforms of Solon (638 BCE - 558 BCE) a century before. While scholars debate the actual conditions of how this consultation may have occurred, it cannot be contested that ancient Greek law influenced Roman law given that the Italian peninsula had Greek communities well before the *Law of the Twelve Tables*. In fact, the coastal areas in Southern Italy were referred to as *Magna Graecia* (Greater Greece). It is not hard to imagine that their legal practices permeated throughout Italy.

The Law of the Twelve Tables was enshrined and displayed on twelve bronze tables in the Roman Forum. While the original artifacts are lost, their content has survived in fragments and through what has been relayed by various secondary sources. The Law instituted several legal rights and the legal status of citizens. It consisted of the following:

- As in the *mos maiorum*, family and property ownership were noted as basic to societal cohesion. Clarifications were cited between property ownership and squatters' rights. It determined that contracts should be written and witnessed in cases of property sales/transfers. Given Rome's agricultural heritage, this part of the law was important.

- Crimes and their punishments were identified, such as robbery, false swearing and destruction of property.
- Family inheritances and guardianship rules were established. The role of the *paterfamilias* was limited to his own immediate family, which was a significant change. As a strike back at the plebeians, the law prevented the intermarriage between patricians and plebeians. This shortsightedness festered after the establishment of the *Law of the Twelve Tables* and was repealed soon after its publication.
- The legal justice system was opened to all citizens equally. Out-of-court settlement was encouraged, but if not possible legal proceedings were permitted. The death penalty was made more difficult to acquire under the law. The ancient practice of ostracizing was memorialized. Defaulting on debts was considered a serious crime.
- The law abolished the division between patrician and plebeian by reorienting to those having property and those without property. The term *proletarii* (laborer) was used for those citizens without land.

The extraordinary powers granted to the *decemvirate* made their promulgations absolute and not subject to appeal by any governmental body. They were only subject to assent by the *comitia centuriata*, who ultimately approved of the law. This action was the start of the formal constitutional process of Republican Rome.

In 449 BCE, the Roman government resumed its prior working by restoring the *consuls* as supreme executive leaders of the Roman state, but their absolute sovereignty was abdicated. Tribunes were made *sacrosanctus* (inviolate), which meant that their person was protected by the state and any injury committed by another was punishable by ostracizing.

The plebeian assemblies (*consilium plebis)* gained equal power to the *comitia centuriata*. The tribunes were given veto powers against consular resolutions. These additional powers granted to the plebeians are known at the Valerian-Horatian Laws and were meant to curtail what appeared to be, and in many cases were, arbitrary judgments by the magistracies. The patricians no longer held absolute power which was the basis for the constitutional reforms, but while the law inaugurated a significant improvement to plebeian rights (hailed as the second founding of Rome), the plebeians continued to fight for more political clout. The direct conflict simmered down, but the class struggle would be a *status quo* of Republican Rome for generations to come. Regardless, the institutions of government were then inscribed. While certain aspects of the law would change periodically, the Roman legal code was instituted.

These legal institutions, in one form or another, have influenced other legal codes that remain in effect to date. When contemplated, this influence that has lasted for over 2,000 years is quite astonishing. The Ancient Romans' encoding of their traditions into a legal system is as much a testimony to their passion for justice as it was their ability to innovate practices previously stemming from civilizations such as the Ancient Greeks and Babylonians. Their influence is such that Max Radin can easily point out that, "The Roman Law is a body of rules that governed the social relations of many peoples in Europe, Asia and Africa for some period between the earliest prehistoric times and 1453 CE, or even to the present time, and we might include America in the territory concerned."[27] Modern civil and common law have taken their influences directly from Roman law. Subsequent cultures have modified it since Roman times, such as those in Europe through the Medieval Period, and culminating under English law.

Any treatise on Roman law cannot ignore the fact that ancient Roman society had slavery as one of its important societal components, as had many other societies influenced by Roman law including the English colonies in America and then the United States prior to the Emancipation Proclamation in 1863 CE by Abraham Lincoln, later consummated in 1865 CE as the Thirteenth Amendment to the United States Constitution. While slavery can be easily ascribed as a social evil, Roman law was not blind to the rights of slaves. Having no personal freedom or property rights, Roman slaves were protected by law against abuse and they had a distinct legal path to freedom where they could then possess similar rights as free persons. This is a significant distinction from slave treatment in other societies. We also cannot ignore

---

[27] Max Radin, *Fundamental Concepts of the Roman Law* (California Law Review, 12, 6: September 24), 396.

the fact that in Roman society, as in Ancient Greece, only men had what we now consider full rights as a free citizen. Women, children, foreigners and slaves had less legal rights than men.

If the Romans and other ancient cultures before them limited total freedom to men only, where did they get their concepts of ethics? Gill points out that, "One of the most important features of contemporary ethical philosophy has been the revival of virtue ethics, of a type that is often explicitly influenced by Greco-Roman model…" To understand this, modern readers cannot use a current understanding of ethical models as a guide, but need to look at how the ancients thought of virtue and moral belief. Deriving from the Greeks, Roman thinkers looked back to the ethical arguments of Aristotle and the Stoics. The Stoics placed their confidence in the rational aspect of human consciousness, so to control one's emotions, therefore, to understand right and wrong and thus create orderly behavior, to discipline oneself and act accordingly, was important. They viewed virtue as self-control of the will in alignment with nature. This applied to slave and free men, but only certain men were endowed with such gifts.

Cicero (Marcus Tullius Cicero 106 BCE - 43 BCE) and Seneca (Lucius Annaeus Seneca 4 BCE - 65 CE) were Roman thinkers and proponents of the Stoic philosophy. Whereas Aristotle relied on a nurturing process for human nature through reason, which makes one properly disciplined. Once disciplined, they can pursue perfecting wisdom and intellect. This way appears to be more reliant on chance and somewhat elitist as only philosophers could achieve the highest order of human ethical authority. While deeply respecting Aristotle, the pragmatic Romans appear to have been persuaded more by the Stoic order of self-discipline than by Aristotle's nurturing path. This self-discipline translated into the Roman sense of law, order and what constituted a virtuous life. Woven into this principle was the Roman's belief that only a virtuous man could handle the benefits of full freedom and administer rightness to those within his purview.

The Romans further believed in the right ordering of society through the concept of justice as an ideal state. While in their view men were the appropriate arbiters of this order, it does not minimize the importance of the administration of justice in society. This is a fundamental legacy that the Romans bequeathed to subsequent generations. Cicero, an influential Roman stoic, firmly believed that the primary function of civic duty was the proper dispensing of justice, morality and principles. Maas is explicit when he determines, "No concept is so closely tied to the political society as that of justice, which, according to Cicero's definition of *civitas*, distinguishes it from any other gathering."[28]

Cicero's definition of *civitas* is the combination of citizens and their legal organization. This is what we today call government. He believed that human beings, through reason and in communion with their fellow citizens, produced an environment of justice which could only be destroyed by moral failure. His political philosophy involved all members of society contributing to the order of justice and spreading its merits by venerating the law through subsequent generations. This is the necessary essence in the creation, unity and maintenance of a principled state. Therefore, a principled state can engage in healthy deliberation, enact changes and improvements without destroying itself in self-defeating conflicts. Cicero warned that a moral dissolution of a state's core beliefs is dangerous to its well-being and leads to its corruption and downfall. Additionally, he advised against the adulation of riches as a harmful distraction from embracing what is virtuous. He believed virtue was the soul of the state and it becomes corrupt by the blind pursuit of fortune. These are remarkable admonitions to the modern, Western world.

Much to the surprise of modern readers, even the Roman Emperors were serious students of ancient literature, philosophy, history and the law. These influences penetrated all levels of Roman society, including the emperors who were mostly consumed by the affairs of state, politics and military matters. Tiberius Caesar (42 BCE - 37 CE), the heir of Augustus (63 BCE - 14 CE), is credited with establishing several libraries throughout Rome. Suetonius (Gaius Suetonius Tranquillus, 69 CE - 122 CE), a celebrated Roman historian, acknowledges that Tiberius was a student of Theodorus of Gadara, a 1st century BCE Greek rhetorician. Houston notes that, "Tiberius was, in short, a man trained and active in literature and scholarly matters like so many men of his

---

[28] Richard W. Maass, *Political Society and Cicero's Ideal State* (Historical Methods, 45, 2: April-June 2012), 84.

class and time."[29]   Rome's leaders and ruling classes were deeply ingrained with the study and application of law. It was important to them to provide and maintain the moral order based upon prior generations of ancient thought and practices. This kind of depth escapes the imagination of modern society where Roman emperors are often portrayed in popular culture as small-minded despots bent on self-indulgence, ambition and power.

Many scholars look back at the *Law of the Twelve Tables* and instruct that, while they defined Roman legal practices, they also maintained the power of the patricians in the guise of acquiescing to the plebeians. Albeit a cynical view, Watson observes that, "The patricians retained their monopoly of offices, the code contains only the private law that the patricians were willing to share with the plebeians, and the plebeians still could not know the law because the Twelve Tables did not contain the forms of action. No public or religious law!"[30]   While this may be the case the Romans, whether purposefully or inadvertently, provided Rome and thereafter the world with a legal code that set the standard for legal practices to this very day. This is quite an achievement for an ancient civilization, but if we look earnestly at their motives we can see that the ancient Romans were adamant to apply their core beliefs and vigorously sought to memorialize their way of life. It is clear that their leaders and legislators were learned, passionate men whose intellects were illuminated by deep, philosophical thought directed at providing for the safety, preservation and expansion of an enlightened civilization. In this endeavor, can we hear the echo of words to be written by another group of free-thinking leaders in a future government constitution?

"We the people ... in order to form a more perfect union, establish justice, insure domestic tranquility, provide for the common defense, promote the general welfare, and secure the blessings of liberty to ourselves and our posterity..." (Preamble to the United States Constitution)

---

[29] George W. Houston, *Tiberius and the Libraries: Public Book Collections and Library Buildings in the Early Roman Empire* (Libraries & the Cultural Record, 43, 3: 2008), 248.
[30] Alan. Watson, *Two Early Codes, the Ten Commandments and the Twelve Tables: Causes and Consequences*, (Journal of Legal History, 25, 2: August 2004), 130.

24. Cary, M. and H.H. Scullard. *A History of Rome*. New York: Palgrave Publishers, 1975.
25. LeGlay, Marcel, Jean-Louis Voisin and Yann Le Bohec. *A History of Rome*. West Sussex: Wiley-Blackwell, 2009.
26. Ibid, Marcel, 2009.
27. Radin, Max. *Fundamental Concepts of the Roman Law*. California Law Review: 12, 5 (July 2004). 393-411.
28. Maass, Richard W. *Political Society and Cicero's Ideal State*. Historical Methods: 45, 2 (April-June 2012). 79-9.
29. Houston, George W. *Tiberius and the Libraries: Public Book Collections and Library Buildings in the Early Roman Empire*. Libraries & the Cultural Record: 43, 3 (2008). 247-269.
30. Watson, Alan. *Two Early Codes, the Ten Commandments and the Twelve Tables: Causes and Consequences*. Journal of Legal History: 25, 2 (August 2004) 129-149.

Abatino, Barbara, Giuseppe Dari-Mattiacci, and Enrico C. Perotti. *Depersonalization of Business in Ancient Rome.* Oxford Journal of Legal Studies: 31, 2 (Summer 2011). 365-389.

Berman, Harold J. *The Origins of Western Legal Science.* Harvard Law Review: 90, 5 (March 1977). 894-944.

de Wilde, Marc. *Fides Publica in Ancient Rome and its Reception by Grotius and Locke.* Legal History Review: 79, 3 & 4 (November 2011). 455-487.

Gill, Christopher. *Ancient Thought.* Phronesis: 51, 3 (August 2006). 294-302.

Hadley, James. *Introduction to Roman Law.* Harvard Law Review: 45, 6 (April 1932). 1141.

Klingenberg, Georg. *Penal practice and penal policy in ancient Rome.* Legal History Review: 76, 3 & 4 (September 2008). 393-395.

Neschke-Hentschke, Ada. *The Cambridge History of Greek and Roman Political Thought.* Phronesis: 48, 2 (May 2003). 152-163.

Peachin, Michael. *Roman Law and the Legal World of the Romans.* Mnemosyne: 65, 4 & 5 (2012). 866-868.

Remer, Gary. *The Classical Orator as Political Representative: Cicero and the Modern Concept of Representation.* Journal of Politics: 72, 4 (October 2010).1063-1082.

Sande, Siri. *Life and Art in the Countryside: Happiness and/or Roman Virtue?* Symbolae Osloenses: 85, 1(2011).161-168.

Shiffman, Mark. *Plutarch among the Postcolonialists.* Perspectives on Political Science: 37, 4 (Fall 2008). 223-230.

Youni, Maria S. *Transforming Greek practice into Roman law: manumissions in Roman Macedonia.* Legal History Review: 78, 3 & 4 (November 2010). 311-340.

Chapter III

The *Corpus Juris Civilis* of Byzantine Emperor, Justinian I, and its Impact on European and Western Law

Historiography

Introduction

The Eastern Roman Empire, as the Byzantine Empire, believed itself to be had an astounding 1,000 year history that lasted from when Constantine the Great moved the capital of the Roman Empire from Rome to Constantinople in 324 BCE until its fall to the Ottoman Turks in 1453 CE. While there is no single leader that has embodied Byzantium's historical trajectory, there are several that provoke historical enquiry as to their impact on Byzantine history.

1. Byzantine Historians

Theophanes the Confessor, a Byzantine monk and scholar who lived around 758 BCE, was the first notable historical chronicler of the Byzantine Empire. He assumed the work of previous Roman historians and chronicled events from the reign of Diocletian around 284 BCE through the reign of Michael I Rhangabe in 813 CE. Theophanes' work is considered essential to understanding the periods of the 7th and 8th centuries where other historical accounting is limited. After Theophanes was Joseph Genesius, a pseudo name for an anonymous Byzantine historian who in the 10th century recorded Byzantine history in the same annalistic style as Theophanes and Symeon Logothetes. His chronicles address the period of Emperor Basil I in the 7th century, the Second Iconoclast Period and the Macedonian Dynasty. After Genesius, Leo the Deacon, who lived around 950 CE, chronicled the history of Emperor Nikephoros II Phokas, praising Byzantine military qualities. Later, Nicetas Choniates, a Greek Byzantine government official, composed a history of the Byzantine Empire from the early 1100s to early 1200s. More modern historiographers of the Byzantine Empire are Otto Karl Seeck in the 1920s, who was a German historian and peer of Theodor Mommsen (who helped Seeck's career in acquiring academic credentials). His works focused on Late Antiquity and the Byzantine Empire. John Bagnell Bury, an Irish historian of the Later Roman Empire who objected to the label "Byzantinist" in his preface to his work

Later Roman Empire. He preferred the era being referred to as the Later Roman Empire as in his book title. George Ostrogorsky, a Yugoslavian historian (1902-1976 CE), is a world renowned historian for his Byzantine studies. He was a professor at the University of Belgrade.

2. The Byzantine Empire: Three Major Dynamics

Whether or not the Byzantine Empire fell is not contested by historians. Given their location in the eastern portion of the Roman Empire, there are three major dynamics that would indelibly influence the Byzantine civilization, some of which lead to its ultimate demise:

- Byzantium was embedded in the Hellenistic world and was influenced by Greek culture from the ancient past. The Byzantines eventually abandoned the Latin language for Greek and adopted many important Greek traits such as philosophy, law and art. Despite this, they perceived themselves as fully Roman and so did their rivals.
- The Byzantine Empire found itself in one of the most resource-rich and strategically positioned locations of the Roman Empire. The eastern provinces had vast farming and economic sway. Constantinople was geographically located in Thrace at the mouth of the Black Sea and had ready access to the Aegean and Mediterranean Seas. This gave Byzantium control over maritime activity in the east, naval supremacy and a strongly defensible port.
- Given its Eastern proximity, Byzantium was heavily influenced by Eastern religions and societies. Most notably, Christianity's formation began in the Eastern provinces, emerging from Jerusalem in Judea and spreading through most cities including Antioch in Syria, Ephesus in Anatolia, Constantinople in Thrace and many others before spreading westward. In addition, the Eastern cultures of the Hebrews, Arabs, Turks and others would continue to collide with Byzantium.

It is this last component of the three major dynamics, the clash of different civilizations upon the Byzantine Empire that instigated its fall. The history of Byzantium from its earliest times is the story of the Empire battling outside forces seeking to acquire more land and resources and their willingness to take them by force from Byzantine territories.

From its beginning, Byzantium inherited the frontier wars of ancient Rome; the Byzantine Empire's borders were encroached and attacked by multiple barbarian hordes in the 4th and 5th centuries. The Visigoths, Huns, Alans and Vandals crossed the Rhine and Danube into Western Europe and attempted to push into the Eastern Empire. Justinian I (482-565 CE), also called The Great, is recognized for his attempt to regain the lost territories of the Western Roman Empire. Through his general Belisarius (500-565 CE), Justinian re-conquered Africa pushing out the Vandals. Belisarius also successfully recaptured Italian territories in Sicily, Naples, Ravenna and Rome, effectively pushing back the Goths. The greatness that was Rome's was Justinian's goal. His expansions, however, were short-lived. The Byzantine Empire paid a high price for its Western wars. The wars in the West had meant neglect of the Danube frontiers and the slackening of the imperial struggle against the Persians. In the east, the Persian Empire, Rome's old nemesis, would not abide in its treaties with Byzantium and drove westward taking Syrian territory. Justinian (as would many of his successors) had to fight on both sides of the Empire, costing much treasure and human resources. This weakened the Empire and emboldened their enemies. In the West, the Lombards invaded Italy, taking the Byzantine gains. The Western wars ended in limited success. The Persian threat from the East continued after Justinian's death in 565 CE.

The Persian threat culminated during the reign of Emperor Heraclius (575-641 CE). He fought several cataclysmic wars that ended with the Battle of Nineveh in 627 CE. Heraclius proved an able general and triumphed with the complete decimation of the Persian Empire. This pyrrhic victory was costly because Byzantine resources were severely drained, leaving it in a weak and vulnerable state. With the obsessive defeat of its ancient enemy, the Byzantine Empire lost focus on other potential threats. This was a grave error. It was at this same time that a new power was ascending in the East.

It was after Persia's defeat that the Arab Muslims, under several caliphates from the 7th through the 11th centuries, became a great foe to Byzantium. The Arabs filled the vacuum left by the Persians. Inspired by their new Islamic faith, they ferociously attacked Byzantine territories. In 636 CE, by the Yarmouk River in Syria the Byzantine and Arab forces engaged in battle. The Arabs routed the Byzantine army and claimed Syria as Arabic territory. This battle is a watershed in Arab Muslim hegemony. Due to this victory, their presence in the Levant and Eastern territories expanded greatly and remains to this day. Their success meant the shrinking of Byzantine control in the east and presented new military challenges to contain this substantial threat. Armenia fell in 639 CE and Egypt, one of Byzantium's important farming territories, was lost to the Arabs after several campaigns by 642 CE. Byzantium lost her eastern provinces scarcely ten years after the death of the Prophet Mohammad. Constantinople was laid siege by the Arabs in 674 CE and 717 CE, showing their military prowess, but fortunately for the Byzantines their advances were temporarily repelled.

The Arabs were also successful in taking the key Mediterranean islands of Cyprus in 654 CE and Crete later in 820 CE. They pushed their presence as far as Spain by 711 CE and Southern Italy by 827 CE. These military campaigns and expansion efforts are astounding when considering that at the same time Western Europe was just reforming its leadership after the fall of the Western Roman Empire and the Byzantine Empire was the major hegemony over the prior 300 years. In the short span of 100 years, the Arabs successfully pushed the Byzantines out of the Levant and Egypt, harshly curtailing the Empire's sphere of control.

As in the past, the Byzantine Empire was continually beset by fresh enemies. This period was no different. They had barely quelled several barbarian incursions and local rebellions in the Balkans over the prior centuries. The actions of the Slavs and Bulgars required constant attention. These would keep the Byzantines occupied in the West, while the Arabs held their attention in the East. This was a constant drain on human and material resources. Resulting from failed governmental policies and social conditions that did not satisfy the Empire's substantial needs, the Byzantine Empire often fell short of its full potential and routinely operated from a weakened position. These included a feeble taxation system, deleterious factions between military and noble leadership, inadequate conditions for military recruitment, economic limitations, weak central planning and widespread corruption.

It was under the leadership of Basil II (958-1025 CE) when Byzantium reemerged as a power and regained a measured capacity to fight back against the Arab threat, retaking partial territories in Syria and Mesopotamia and conquering the Bulgarians. His military successes regained Byzantium's footing and held its Western and Eastern adversaries temporarily in check.

Unfortunately, after Basil II's passing, his heir Constantine VII (960-1028 CE) would relinquish many of the internal political successes he had built which were central to Byzantine reemergence. He exhibited poor leadership and cruelty. Among his failures the most destructive was in eliminating Basil's land reforms which further undermined Byzantium's ability to bolster taxes and military recruitment, setting the Empire backwards. Constantine's successor Romanus III (968-1034 CE) further undermined previous tax reforms and allowed the decline of the working class essentially into serfdom under the empowered wealthy classes and large land-owners. The military was greatly weakened while the noble classes enriched themselves. Basil II's re-entrenching efforts quickly evaporated within ten years of his death. This placed the Byzantine Empire in a very precarious position and continued through several emperors after Romanus.

It was not until the reign of Romanus IV (1030-1072 CE) when he realized the detrimental effects that the policies of the prior imperial courts had on the Empire. In the meantime, another new and growing threat faced the Byzantines from the Seljuk Turks. The Seljuks, like the Huns before them, came out of Asia seeking land and wealth. In the 10th century, the Seljuks were converted to Islam and entered Persia by the 11th century, overthrowing a prior Turkish culture. They entrenched themselves in Asia Minor and Syria, taking over previous Arab lands and forming a unified state under the Abbasid Caliphate in 1055 CE.

The Seljuks enacted multiple incursions into Byzantine territory from the beginning of their presence in the region. In 1067 CE, the Seljuks invaded Mesopotamia and Syria. By 1069 CE, the Seljuks assaulted Asia Minor but were repulsed by Romanus IV. Romanus was confident that he could push the Seljuks back, but he underestimated the flagging quality of his armies due to their deterioration under prior regimes. This proved to be a fatal miscalculation. In the meantime, Norman invasions in the West posed a major distraction to Romanus' efforts against the Seljuks. He was forced to abandon the field in 1070 CE, returning to Constantinople. The Seljuks would have to wait. Despite his efforts, the Normans seized Byzantine holdings in Italy, entirely removing their presence on the Italian peninsula. Seeing weakness due to Byzantine losses, and after a failed attempt to conclude a peace treaty concocted by Romanus to mislead them, the Seljuks - led by Alp Arslan (1029-1072 CE) - instead attacked the Byzantines in Asia Minor near the city of Manzikert in 1071 CE.

Romanus, with a reduced force defended Manzikert, but he miscalculated his forces' capabilities and attacked the Seljuks. The Seljuks responded by entrapping the Byzantines, decimating their army. He was betrayed by his rearguard led by Andronicus Doukas, a rival of Romanus who purposely failed to defend the retreating Byzantines, causing the capture of Romanus. In captivity he was forced to make substantial concessions to Alp Arslan. This helped his enemies in Constantinople to undermine his imperial authority. The Doukas family, being rivals of Romanus, secured opposition to Romanus' rule, causing civil war within Byzantium. Doukas eventually prevailed and Romanus was blinded and exiled.

The period following the Battle of Manzikert in 1071 CE began the Byzantine Empire's overall decline for two major reasons. First, the culminated vulnerabilities of the Empire contributed to its defeat in the face of an imminent threat from the Seljuk Turks who became the regional hegemon after the Arabs. Second, the Empire was unable to unite even after the Seljuks sought peace following their victory at Manzikert. Infighting and lack of coordination radically weakened them as a state power. Combined, these two deficiencies left the Byzantine Empire vulnerable to the ongoing incursions of the Turks. The Empire never fully recovered after this battle, leading to its ultimate fall to the Ottoman Empire in 1453 CE. To understand how the Byzantine Empire arrived at this point, it requires a brief review of its more significant leaders and conflicts with regional adversaries.

From here the Byzantine Empire would never again regain the prominence of its earlier days. Constantinople remained a prize for the Turks which in time compelled them to siege the city, leading to its eventual fall in 1453 CE. Fortunately, prior to its fall, many Byzantine scholars, artists and artisans escaped to the West and brought with them the knowledge of the many treasures of the Roman Empire including literature, law, art, architecture and science.

3. Fall of the Byzantine Empire Examined

On May 29, 1453 CE, the Ottoman Empire (Turkish peoples) sacked Constantinople and destroyed forever the last remnants of the Byzantine Empire. Historians do not debate this fact. What may be legitimately examined, however, are when their fall began, the leaders during this period and the factors that brought the Byzantines to their fatal end. Empires do not fall overnight or because of one single event, but due to a confluence of circumstances over time. This was undoubtedly the case for the Byzantine Empire. To this end, there are certain key leaders of the Byzantine Empire that contributed to its historical demise at the hands of the Ottoman Turks in 1453 CE.

Constantine the Great made Christianity the state religion of the Roman Empire. The Edict of Milan in 313 BCE allowed the practice of Christianity, which swiftly made it the dominant religion. Given this, it was of paramount importance to the emperors that controversies were resolved and peace maintained throughout the Roman Empire. This was a significant task of subsequent emperors. Constantine, in order to deal with significant disagreement within the Christian church at that time, called the First Ecumenical Council of Nicaea in 325 BCE. While the church maintained its beliefs and made every effort to claim that it was autonomous to imperial authority, relying on its traditions to resolve internal disputes, it was Constantine that called the first Ecumenical Council to resolve such differences among Christian leaders.

Prior to the Great Schism between the Eastern and Western Christian Churches in 1054 CE, seven such Ecumenical Councils were convoked to maintain order in the state-authorized Christian Church. Constantine co-opted the Christian faith and used its cult to augment the emperor's prestige as God's chosen civil leader and protector of the Christian church and Roman world. The Christian faith was used to advancing and protecting the empire from infidels pouring in from outside. The barbarians in the west and in the east were the Persians and later the Arabs, all of whom were infidels to Christianity. The empire would fight holy wars against the Arabs in the Crusades. The Christian faith provided a commanding rallying point for the Byzantines. This unity supported the empire's need for social, military and economic integration.

What is now known as the Fourth Crusade (1202-1204 CE) was meant to be the retaking of Jerusalem from the "infidels" by the Western powers, but instead it became the demise of Byzantium as the Western crusaders turned and sacked Constantinople. This event was the penultimate disaster for the Byzantine Empire and represented a decline that would lead to its final end. The Fourth Crusade was also the final major effort made by the West to re-conquer the Holy Land. Richard I of England, the Lion Heart negotiated with Saladin to gain passage for Western pilgrims and merchants.

Regarding the Crusades, it was the Fourth Crusade that posed serious challenges to the Western crusaders. There was difficulty in amassing a sizeable army and the much needed safe passage to the east. The Western sovereigns finally negotiated with Venice for a considerable sum. Due to shrinking numbers and a disorganized plan, the West defaulted on its financial commitment to Venice, causing the remaining powers to bargain with Venice by agreeing to recapture the city of Zara for Venice. Despite it being a Christian city, the Venetians led by Doge Enrico Dandolo and crusaders led by Boniface of Montferrat conquered Zara after much debate and resistance from Pope Innocent III. From there, the crusaders marched on toward Constantinople. There, Alexius IV made promises to the crusaders that his father Alexius III would help repay their debt to Venice if they helped him regain the Byzantine throne. This action coupled with Venice's grudge against Byzantium led the crusading army directly at Constantinople.

By April, 1204 CE, after nearly a year of siege, the city fell to the crusaders causing Alexius III to flee. Constantinople was savagely sacked and was stripped of almost every valuable work of art and treasure. The city's precious cultural centers were destroyed, including its famous library, much to the chagrin of the pope who nonetheless was pleased with the subjugation of the Eastern sees to Rome. Despite this, the city was conquered and divided by the Western powers.

The new government was set up under an elected emperor by the Venetians and Franks. Consequently, Count Baldwin of Flanders was crowned emperor of the Latin Empire of Constantinople, but this was not the end of Byzantine rule. After a series of internal conflicts with the Western powers, the Byzantines reclaimed Constantinople in 1216 CE.

The fall of the Byzantine Empire is certainly an important historical fact given their many contributions to Western civilization. Known by the Byzantines themselves as the Eastern Roman Empire it is important to appreciate the proud history of their civilization which shouldered the responsibility of maintaining Roman culture, customs and hegemony after the fall of the Western Roman Empire. Their empire was established by Constantine I in 324 CE and lasted over 1,000 years. Among Western civilizations, its duration is rivaled only by the Western Roman Empire, which lasted nearly as long. This amazing fact is often overshadowed by the considerable attention given to the history of the Roman Republic and Empire over that of the Byzantine Empire. Their relative obscurity results also from the limited resources available on their empire.

4. Conclusion

The civil unrest that followed the Battle of Manzikert in 1071 CE and the incursion by the Crusaders devastated the Byzantine Empire. The ascension of the Seljuks and the loss of Anatolia further degraded their hegemony. They were no longer seen as invincible. While Byzantium lasted another 400 years, it would do so in a severely weakened state leading to its final collapse in 1453 CE. The effects of inadequate governmental policies, social upheavals, debasement of its currency, reduced tax revenues, failed military recruitment, an impoverished working class, the recklessness and ambitions of its emperors, corruption and constant withering attacks from its enemies, all contributed to Byzantium's end. It was at this moment, after the Battle of Manzikert, that we begin to see the overall decline of the Byzantine Empire. Their legacy continued, however, because of its many cultural achievements and preservations. While the Byzantine Empire fell, all was not lost in that the Byzantines advanced the progress of the Ancient Greeks and

Romans, adding their own brand of culture found in the many works of art, Christian philosophy and architecture found in Byzantium. They also succeeded in preserving Western philosophy and law, which are the foundations for modern Europe and Western Civilization.

Background

Justinian I (482-565 CE), a Byzantine emperor, considering himself and his empire fully Roman, began in 529 CE - with the assistance of seventeen eminent jurists led by Tribonian (485-547 CE) - to consolidate and standardize Roman law into what is known as the *Corpus Juris Civilis* (Justinian Code). We will examine the impetus and development of the *Corpus Juris Civilis* and its subsequent impact on early European law and later Western law and civilization.

Preceding the Byzantines, the ancient Roman legal system was developed in prehistory beginning within Etruscan religious practices. It continued to evolve through the Roman monarchy, the establishment of the patricians and the political struggles of the plebeians against the Roman social hierarchy. These efforts culminated in the establishment of the *Lex Romana* (Roman law) which directed civil, government and military affairs throughout the Roman Republic and Empire for over a millennium.

During Rome's seminal period where concepts of law and justice matured, significant portions of the Italian peninsula were known as *Magna Graecia* (Latin for Greater Greece), where many influences of Ancient Greece abounded, especially Ancient Greek law. The flourishing Roman culture combined with Ancient Greek civilization to form Roman society and a unique legal code.

Given that Ancient Greek culture and it customs greatly influenced Roman society, it is equally important to pause and consider the naissance of Ancient Greek law to discover how it was derived and why it took root so effectively within Roman society.

As we've established some historians assert that the need for military defense caused democracy to begin. Examining Ancient Greece, it was the Greek *polis* (city-state) that conscripted most of its male citizens as armed defenders who were called the hoplites. Hoplites were citizen-soldiers. Vasillopulos, states that, "...hoplites were a cause of the extension of full political participation for a major part of the Athenian citizenry...."[31] It seems that the impetus for citizens to rally and defend their city provided a significant opportunity to meet, speak of common concerns and work to address and resolve issues once service was completed. It fostered the right environment for democratic ideals but, this was not the sole reason for their development. Vasillopulos further adds, "While the hoplite phalanx could not guarantee the development of democracy, neither could economic change no matter how pervasive, nor political philosophy no matter how profound."[32] So an important addition to this is that Athenian society was built on the "rule of law" and the concept of equal rights for all citizens. Athens was the civic center of the Athenians' lives. Citizens worked both in the city and throughout the countryside farming or performing city labor. Athenians were united by their self-governance; defended their city-state, supplied goods and worshiped the gods together as fundamental underpinnings of their society. These concepts were readily adopted by the Romans who if nothing else are well-known for their ability to assimilate foreign cultures and traditions.

As discussed earlier, Rome, even before its Greek influences had a solid legal foundation deriving from its Etruscan predecessors. Ancient Rome was a deeply moral and principled culture steeped in religion and based upon a solid foundation of social customs and traditions. In its seminal period, before Rome established itself as a firm polity, these social customs were unwritten, but deeply rooted in their tribal norms, mores and folkways. These customs are known in Latin as the *mos maiorum* or ancestral customs, literally "custom (way) of our ancestors (elders)." Although unwritten, the *mos maiorum* provided the moral inspiration that propelled disparate tribes to gather and flourish into one of the greatest civilizations of the ancient world and one that would also shape future societies.

It is from the Ancient Roman society that the Byzantine Empire would initially inherit its civilization and identity. Constantine I (Roman Emperor, 272-337 CE) moved the capital of the Roman Empire from Rome to Byzantium - a Greek colony that was later named

---

[31] Christopher Vasillopulos, *The Nature of Athenian Hoplite Democracy* (Armed Forces & Society, 22, 1: Fall 1995), 49-63.
[32] Ibid. Vasillopulos, 53.

Constantinople - in 324 CE. Constantinople's location not only moved the Roman Empire's imperial seat from the west to the east geographically, but placed the city directly within the Eastern Roman Empire which at that time was broadly Greek influenced and largely Greek speaking. The Roman Empire at its height called this province Thrace located at the mouth of the Black Sea where the city of Constantinople was situated.

Constantinople was a large and wealthy city and the birthplace of what is now called the Byzantine Empire, a name given well after its fall in 1453 CE to the Ottoman Turks. As inheritors of the Roman Empire and after the fall of the Western Roman Empire, the Byzantines saw themselves as wholly Roman and they called themselves Romans until their end. Through Late Antiquity, the Byzantine Empire was the strongest and most influential European civilization when considering its military, economic and cultural hegemony.

Attributed to Justinian I, with the prolific leadership of Tribonian, was the momentous charge of gathering all prior legal codes, compiling such material, removing duplication and editing these laws into one cogent legal codex. Lawful edicts since the time of Emperor Hadrian (117 CE - 138 CE) were gathered. Sources also included the *Codex Gregorianus* (constitutions and edicts of Roman emperors between 130 CE and 290 CE), the *Codex Hermogenianus* (constitutions from the first tetrarchy of Diocletian between 293 CE and 294 CE) and the *Codex Theodosianus* to be discussed further. Tribonian had Justinian's full confidence and was recognized for his exceptional intellectual and organizational skills.

Between 529 CE and 535 CE, Justinian I commissioned a distinguished panel of jurists presided over by Tribonian to regulate Roman law into a systematic, organized and useable format. Prior to this, Roman law was a disparate accumulation of established laws, judicial outcomes and case precedence from over 1,000 years of practice within the Roman Empire, including the more recent *Codex Theodosianus* (Theodosian Code) completed in 438 CE. This was not the first time a Byzantine emperor had undertaken such a monumental task, but Justinian's became the quintessential legal standard for centuries to come.

One hundred years before, in 429 CE, and for nearly a decade thereafter, Theodosius II (401-450 CE), the co-emperor of Valentinian III (419-455 CE) also attempted to codify Roman law into what is known as the *Codex Theodosianus*. Theodosius' efforts were the first since the *Law of the Twelve Tables* of Republican Rome to collect, organize and publish existing laws. The *Twelve Tables* were the foundation of the *Constitution of the Roman Republic* proceeding from ancient Roman customs known as the *mos maiorum*. Completed in 449 BCE, the *Twelve Tables* memorialized Roman legal customs in writing and were displayed at the time on twelve tables for citizens to read giving its name.

Theodosius was motivated because of what he perceived as a lack of legal skills within the Byzantine Empire. While the effort was largely successful, it was deemed incomplete. Due to the scope of the project Theodosius decided to regress only as far as Constantine I (272-337 CE), limiting it to existing laws (known as *leges* in Roman law) and to not include judicial interpretations and case precedence (known as *ius* in Roman law). A complete historical legal collection would remain a pressing challenge to the Byzantine Empire until Justinian. According to Tate, Justinian's Code acknowledges that, "...its aim was to edit the Theodosian Code and its two Diocletianic predecessors so that they might be combined with later constitutions in a fourth code that would replace them all."[33] From this, it appears that Justinian had more complete sources to draw from than is extant today. The author goes on to acknowledge that Justinian's Code is recognized not so much for reforming ancient laws, but making them into a uniform procedural codex.

Justinian and Tribonian deemed it important for the legal professions to not only interpret ratified laws, but allow for legal interpretation to be represented as a classical characteristic of law practice. To this end, the *Corpus Juris Civilis* is divided into four major components: 1) the *Codex* - containing imperial pronouncements having the force of law, 2) the *Digesta* - memorializing juridical works, existing legal opinions and scholarly interpretations of the law, 3) the *Institutiones* - the training

---

[33] Joshua C. Tate, *Codification of Late Roman Inheritance Law: Fideicommissa and the Theodosian Code* (Legal History Review, 76, 3&4: September 2008), 239.

manuals for jurists and legal students and 4) *Novellae* - comprising new laws at that time.

Each of these components made the *Corpus Juris Civilis* a unique work and an improvement over the *Codex Theodosianus*, because it not only incorporated the entire history of Roman law known at that time, but included case law that provided interpretive support traditionally used in legal practice even today. Underscoring this advancement, Naumovski, et al. comment that:

"The importance of the *Digest* [*Digesta*], as a central dimension of the codification is in the enlightenment of all institutes of pre-Justinian, i.e. classical law. The main characteristic of the *Digest* is also the presentation of specific cases, as examined by classical jurisprudence. In this way the aim of the *Digest* is successful application as well as harmonization of these institutes....."[34]

The *Digest* offered an innovative approach by organizing volumes of sometimes conflicting laws into a unified arrangement. The Justinian Code (also known as the *Codex Justinianus* in Latin) was published in both Latin and Greek, making it very relevant to the then current legal community. Having such an organized legal code reinforced the centralized Byzantine authority. This legal code ruled on most aspects of Byzantine dealings: state, public, private, individual, family, citizens, non-citizens and business.

One of the major factors that make Justinian's Code different than the Roman law is that it also incorporated the Christian worldview. Christian morality, philosophy and ethics were a hefty consideration for Justinian and Byzantine society as they interpreted and applied Roman law. What is also clear is that the Code was not simply an organizational improvement over prior Roman law, but it was updated to include existing Hellenistic culture and customs found throughout Byzantium. In this, we begin to see Christian influences on law demonstrating a greater benevolence than Roman law.

On the other hand, given Byzantium's adoption of Christianity at the state level, this also meant that Justinian's Code was exclusively

---

[34] Goce Naumovski, Mirjana Polenak-Akimovska, and Vasko Naumovski, *Roman Law and the Foundations of Contemporary Sports Law: The Approach of Justinian's Legisltaion* (Research in Kinesiology, 39, 2: 2011), 198.

Christian and did not include legal protections for non-Christians. Brewer et al. identify that Justinian's legal policy toward the Jews is summarized in a section of the Code promulgated in 527 CE. It essentially defined someone as a heretic who did not proclaim faith with the Orthodox Catholic Church; therefore, Christian heretics, pagans and Jews were all considered foreigners to the Byzantine state and not fully protected under its laws.[35] Expressions of freedom and equality were limited to those professing the Christian faith, but non-Christians often did not have access to such ideals. Additionally, improving slave standards was totally overlooked by the new code. The slave treatment of rural working populations was provided legal sanction under the law. With regard to the Byzantine state in particular, the Code bolstered the powers of the emperor through its legal justification of the monarchy.

The importance of Justinian's Code was a result of the very real need of the Byzantine courts to administer the law in the absence of accessible, useable information from the sometimes vague and disparate historical sources. To gauge the scope and efficiency of the undertaking, Justinian's Code reduced all prior legal materials from approximately three million sentences to one-hundred fifty thousand contained within in fifty books. According to Holmes:

"Among these were to be found all the matter required to enlighten the hesitating lawyer as to official duties, judicial functions, pledges, contracts, usury, nuptials, wills and codicils, legacies and trusts, relations of slaves and freemen, heirship, intestacy [estate distribution without a will], liabilities of those occupying land…crimes and punishments…public works, and miscellaneous definitions."[36]

Given the size of the task and the confusion caused by centuries of partial edits, comments and abbreviations, Justinian prohibited the use of commentaries on the new code so as not to dilute its clarity. Justinian reserved all questions of interpretation to himself as the absolute legislator of Byzantine law.

Nearly 200 years later, Leo III (Byzantine emperor, 717-741 CE) updated the civil and criminal law components of the Justinian Code in

---

[35] Catherine Brewer, *The Status of the Jews in Roman Legislation: The Reign of Justinian 527-565 CE* (European Judaism, 38, 2: Autumn 2005), 128.
[36] William Gordon Holmes, *The Age of Justinian and Theodora: A History of the 6th Century A.D.* (Charles River Editors: 2011), 800.

726 CE. This legal manual is called the *Ecloga*. It was meant to simplify and modernize certain aspects of the Justinian Code and boldly included additional Christian moral ethics regarding the family and providing equality for all people. In contrast, we begin to see how Eastern cultures influenced Byzantium at this time because certain penal mutilations were also introduced, including: blinding, amputation of the hand and or leg, cutting off the nose and or tongue, castration and other before unseen practices. These were likely imported from their Eastern neighbors who had such practices as inspired by the ancient Code of Hammurabi that called for an "eye for an eye" as penal retribution. To be fair, these methods may have been seen as more humane than the death penalty, but stiffer than monetary fines.

The *Ecloga* was also a tool used by Leo to show the Byzantines that he was a serious reformer of corruption which became a consistent theme for Byzantine emperors. Leo is most noted for Iconoclasm which led Byzantium into one of its greatest internal conflicts. Iconoclasm, a popular cult in the Eastern Church was ultimately defeated. It held that it was heretical to venerate religious icons or visages. These two developments reveal how significantly Eastern civilizations impacted the Byzantine Empire.

George Ostrogorsky observes that, "In the Byzantine Empire, Roman law remained the basis of legal development throughout its history, and Justinian's *Corpus* was the starting point for all future work in this field."[37] After the collapse of the Western Roman Empire it was the Byzantines who preserved the classical Roman legal system for future generations. Roman law was lost in the West due to the vacuum of political power and leadership, not to be revived until its use by the Holy Roman Emperor Frederick I Barbarossa (1122-1190 CE) 500 years later.

It was through the reconstitution of Western powers including the Franks, Germans and the burgeoning wealth of the Italian city-states such as Venice and Genoa that enabled the West to again embrace the study of classical law. Due to the Byzantines' efforts, the Justinian Code was preserved. Law scholars refreshed its application in the West, most

---

[37] George Ostrogorsky, *History of the Byzantine State* (New Brunswick, NJ: Rutgers University Press, 1969), 77.

notably at the law school in Bologna, Italy, that later became Europe's first university.

Frederick I assumed his empire as the Justinian Code was resurging in Western Europe. It helped Frederick to effectively manage the Western Roman Empire in the same organized manner much as the Romans and Byzantines had done. Like Justinian, Frederick used the Code to justify his lordship over Germany and Italy and legitimize monarchical sovereignty as different from and superior to papal authority.

Prior to Frederick, the Papacy prevailed against the Western kings in what is known as the Investiture Controversy. The Papacy fought with Western monarchies over the right to invest bishops and abbots throughout the 11th and 12th centuries. Western leaders claimed the "divine right of kings" over papal authority. Papal authority, however, prevailed. The Roman Catholic Church's success resulting from the Investiture Controversy, much like the Justinian Code did in Byzantium, consolidated Western powers under the banner of Christianity, thus forming the Holy Roman Empire. The Justinian Code balanced this power by providing a legal framework for Frederick's imperial aspirations, thus giving Frederick the concept that he was the legitimate inheritor and successor to Imperial Rome like Charlemagne (748-814 CE) did before him.

Frederick's resurrection of the Justinian Code helped improve feudalism, the prevailing European political system. Feudalism was a remnant from the collapse of the Western Roman Empire and dominated Medieval Europe for over 500 years. So while the sovereigns of Europe continued to bolster their legitimacy using the legacies of Roman law, the masses abided under the system of feudal law. Feudal law was essentially a gathering of civil laws and military practices taken from Germanic customs and cannon law (church law) practiced in Europe, whereby strong and prosperous land owners managed property and labor in service to country and king. The land owners, usually legally recognized by the king, were considered nobles who carried a specific level of authority, title and rank for services rendered. In turn, nobles had vassals who took oaths of fealty and peasants that managed their property and land, both in service to the noble. These were called fiefs, a word derived from the Latin term *fuedum*. Madden relays that, "...the law codes of the Lombards, the Burgundians, and the Salian Franks provided a civilizing legal bridge between the fall of the Western Empire and the more westernized law codes that would follow in the later Middle Ages."[38] These reciprocal relationships prevailed in Europe from approximately 900 CE to1800 CE in various forms. After 1500 CE, feudalism waned considerably.

Justinian's Code continued to influence continental European law throughout the Feudal Period with the engine of academic law centers. England was not as principally influenced as the continental European states because it had already developed its own legal standards by the time the Justinian Code was revived. England produced its own laws called common law. However, it must be noted that English law was likely shaped by Roman law, given its earliest lawgivers, such as Edward the Confessor (1005-1066 CE) who, in his early years, received much of his legal knowledge during his exile in continental Europe and conveyed such experiences to England when he became its ruler in 1042 CE.

Feudalism in England was dramatically altered after the adoption of the *Magna Carta* in 1215 CE, when nobles sought additional rights from the king, especially regarding land ownership. By 1645 CE, England's Parliament effectively abolished feudalism and adopted many of the practices borrowed from the legacies of Roman law. Parallel to developments in continental Europe, English feudalism began to wane due to the obvious shortfalls in legal clarity under English common law and European feudal law. Additionally, Enlightenment thinkers began to stimulate notions of natural rights, which expanded the scope of both common and civil law. Simonds observes that, "John Locke's chapter on property in the Second Treatise of Government undermines the feudal theory of tenure and liegnancy prevailing in English law and restores classical allodial [property rights without a landlord] natural property rights to all individuals."[39]

By the end of the 17th century, the idea of natural rights permeated Enlightenment-Age philosophy and found its way into the legal concepts

---

[38] M. Stuart Madden, *Paths of Western Law after Justinian* (Widener Law Journal, 22, 3: 2013), 758.
[39] Roger T. Simonds, *John Locke's Use of Classical Legal Theory* (International Journal of the Classical Tradition, 3, 4: Spring 1997), 424.

of human rights, self-evident and inalienable rights of humanity that were not provided by any person, sovereign or legal system, but are universal and freely inherent in human existence. It is the British Enlightenment thinker John Locke (1632-1704 CE) with whom is primarily attributed the inspiration of the Declaration of Independence. He is noted for his assertion that natural rights include life, liberty and property. One has the right to liberty as long as another's life is not violated to gain it, and one has the right to property as long as another's liberty is not violated to gain it. This was viewed as a social contract among all human beings living within a system of shared laws that protect these rights. These models greatly affected the thoughts and works of Thomas Jefferson, John Adams, James Madison and other framers of the United States Constitution.

France, under Napoleon Bonaparte, improved France's legal reforms begun during the French Revolution by drafting a sweeping legal reform known as the Napoleonic Code in 1804 CE that fully replaced prior feudal laws. The Napoleonic Code strongly emphasized the concept of "rule of law" which holds that laws should govern states, not subjective rulings by individuals. The concept of "rule of law" is a common thread between the continental European and English legal systems. The Napoleonic Code, while not replacing the Justinian Code, is its more modern progeny. Wijfells identifies that, "Throughout the First Empire [France] and the 19th century, the stability of the Civil Code (Napoleonic Code) was almost axiomatic as France evolved from one constitutional regime to another."[40]

So, as illustrated here, legal codes and the systems they guide are a significant underpinning for society. While France rapidly changed throughout several tumultuous, evolutionary periods, its Civil Code remained a stabilizing and guiding force. This tradition, handed down from the Greeks and Romans, spread throughout Europe and was transported along with its emigrants to the New World.

The United States of America, at the drafting of its Constitution, incorporates both the common law of England and civil law as separately

---

[40] Alain Wijffels, *Tampering with the Code Civil 1804-2004* (Legal History Review, 72, 3/4: September 2004), 197.

generated from Roman law through the Justinian and Napoleonic Codes. United States law contains five major components:

1. **Common law** - inherited from English common law, where decisions regarding legal matters are decided by judges through court decisions, even where laws and/or regulations may be lacking.
2. **Statutory law** - derived from legislatures or legislators. Statutes can originate from federal, state or local governments.
3. **Administrative regulations** - provided by administrative agencies authorized by legislatures or legislators that serve in their place.
4. **Treaties** - international agreements made between government officials or authorized representatives.
5. **Constitutional law** - the chief legal code contained within the United States Constitution regarding federal, state and individual rights and governmental authority.

The United States' Code (U.S. law) is the precursor to what is now generally recognized as Western law. Western law is the embodiment of traditions handed down from Greek law, Roman law, and English common law, including Judeo-Christian moral philosophy. Western law also embraces the later conceptions of natural law and the "rule of law" derived from Enlightenment thinkers, revolutionaries in the United States and France, humanists of the Renaissance, and from eminent legal scholars and jurists beginning in the Medieval Period. These traditions comprise Western law.

Western law has been a basis for democracy, which propounds these ideals and makes Western law a model for human rights, equality and freedom. Discussing the merits of the United States Constitution, Berger stipulates that the American law system is a "...unique system of separated and divided powers...created to provide internal checks and produce the balance that has given us an ordered liberty unparalleled in history."[41] These very theories were championed by Montesquieu (1689-1755 CE), the French Enlightenment philosopher.

The authors of the United States Constitution devised this model of government by deliberating on prior forms of law and built something

---

[41] Warren E. Burger, *Tell the Story of Freedom* (ABA Journal, 72, 5: May 1986), 54.

completely new. They created a legal system and a government not of laws that justify the ruling classes, but a government comprising the people whom it serves. Consider the Preamble of the United States Constitution:

> "We the People…in order to form a more perfect union, establish justice, insure domestic tranquility, provide for the common defense, promote the general welfare, and secure the blessings of liberty to ourselves and our posterity…"

The foundations of Western law are often the goals of many nations, which include: limited and balanced governmental powers, civil and individual liberty, free economic markets, and self-determination that empower citizens over governments. Gouvernor Morris (1725-1816 CE), a Framer of the U.S. Constitution, is attributed by James Madison the following quote:

"[I] came here as a Representative of America (to the Constitutional Convention); [I] flattered [myself], [I] came here in some degree as a Representative of the whole human race; for the whole human race will be affected by the proceedings of this Convention."[42]

The Justinian Code has certainly had a tremendous impact on Western culture and civilization. It is based in classical Western thought begun by the Greeks, mastered by the Romans, preserved by the Byzantines and adopted throughout Western history. It is not because the law is well-written that it derives such long-lasting power and influence; rather, it is because it reflects and embodies the aspirations of humanity, its soul so to speak, while at the same time, providing an avenue for their pursuit and attainment. Lawgivers throughout the history of Western civilization knew this well and used Western law to promote the rights of humanity within the frameworks of ordered societies.

---

[42] James Madison's Notes of the Constitutional Convention, Consulted November 6, 2014, http://www.consource.org/document/james-madisons-notes-of-the-constitutional-convention-1787-7-5/

31. Vasillopulos, Christopher. *The Nature of Athenian Hoplite Democracy*. Armed Forces & Society: 22, 1 (Fall 1995). 49-63.

32. Ibid, Vasillopulos, 53.

33. Tate, Joshua C. *Codification of Late Roman Inheritance Law: Fideicommissa and the Theodosian Code*. Legal History Review: 76, 3&4 (September 2008). 239.

34. Naumovski, Goce, Mirjana Polenak-Akimovska and Vasko Naumovski. *Roman Law and the Foundations of Contemporary Sports Law: The Approach of Justinian's Legislation*. Research in Kinesiology: 39, 2 (2011). 198.

35. Brewer, Catherine. *The Status of the Jews in Roman Legislation: The Reign of Justinian 527-565 CE*. European Judaism: 38, 2 (Autumn 2005). 128.

36. Holmes, William Gordon. *The Age of Justinian and Theodora: A History of the 6th Century A.D.* Charles River Editors (2011). 800.

37. Ostrogorsky, George. *History of the Byzantine State*. New Brunswick, NJ: Rutgers University Press (1969). 77.

38. Madden, M. Stuart. *Paths of Western Law after Justinian*. Widener Law Journal: 22, 3 (2013). 758.

39. Simonds, Roger T. *John Locke's Use of Classical Legal Theory*. International Journal of the Classical Tradition: 3, 4 (Spring 1997). 424.

40. Wijffels, Alain. *Tampering with the Code Civil 1804-2004*. Legal History Review: 72, 3/4 (September 2004). 197.

41. Burger, Warren E, *Tell the Story of Freedom*. ABA Journal: 72, 5 (May 1986). 54.

42. James Madison's Notes of the Constitutional Convention, Consulted November 6, 2014. http://www.consource.org/document/james-madisons-notes-of-the-constitutional-convention-1787-7-5/

Chapter III - Works Consulted

Burger, Warren E. *Tell the Story of Freedom*. ABA Journal: 72, 5 (May 1986). 54-57.

Brewer, Catherine. *The Status of the Jews in Roman Legislation: The Reign of Justinian 527-565 CE*. European Judaism: 38, 2 (Autumn 2005). 127-139.

de Jong, Hylkje. *A Byzantine Interpretation of D. 12,1,32 and Similar Digest Fragments*. Legal History Review: 80, 1&2 (March 2012). 47-76.

Duggan, Anne J. *Roman, Canon and Common Law in Twelfth-Century England: The Council of Northampton (1164) Re-examined*. Historical Research: 83, 221 (August 2010). 379-408.

Holmes, William Gordon. *The Age of Justinian and Theodora: A History of the 6th Century A.D.* Charles River Editors (2011).

James Madison's Notes of the Constitutional Convention, consulted November 6, 2014. http://www.consource.org/document/james-madisons-notes-of-the-constitutional-convention-1787-7-5/

Madden, M. Stuart. *Paths of Western Law after Justinian*. Widener Law Journal: 22, 3 (2013).   757-828.

Naumovski, Goce, Mirjana Polenak-Akimovska and Vasko Naumovski. *Roman Law and the Foundations of Contemporary Sports Law: The Approach of Justinian's Legislation*. Research in Kinesiology: 39, 2 (2011). 197-201.

Ostrogorsky, George. *History of the Byzantine State*. New Brunswick, NJ: Rutgers University Press (1969).

Shepherd, Gary K. *While Emperor Justinian I Revived Byzantine Splendor at Home, Count Belisarius Revived Its Power Abroad*. Military History: 14, 17 (March 1998). 20-23.

Simonds, Roger T. *John Locke's Use of Classical Legal Theory*. International Journal of the Classical Tradition: 3, 4 (Spring of 1997). 424-433.

Stathakopoulos, Dionysios. *The Elusive Eastern Empire*. History Today: 58, 11 (November 2008). 38-45.

Tate, Joshua C. *Codification of Late Roman Inheritance Law: Fideicommissa and the Theodosian Code*. Legal History Review: 76, 3&4 (September 2008). 237-248.

Vasillopulos, Christopher. *The Nature of Athenian Hoplite Democracy*. Armed Forces & Society: 22, 1 (Fall 1995). 49-63.

Wijffels, Alain. *Tampering with the Code Civil 1804-2004*. Legal History Review: 72, 3/4, (September 2004). 195-214.

Chapter IV

Law in Medieval Europe after the Collapse of the Western Roman Empire

Historiography

Introduction

European society was equally affected by the pen and the sword; however, the sword determined the key geographic and religious tolerance boundaries that designated Europe's geopolitical landscape to this day, which makes the sword most prominent. The Medieval Period or Middle Ages is most attributed to the period from the 5th to 15th centuries. However, the period of the Reformation (1500-1650 CE) and the Peace of Westphalia in 1648 CE conclude foundations of the Middle Ages, making way to the future of Europe through the Renaissance, Enlightenment and the Scientific Age.

1. Historians of Medieval Europe

Much of medieval history was derived from either chronicles (chronologies) or annals of historical figures and/or events. Much of the discipline of the historians of antiquity was lost after the Western Roman Empire declined. Conversely, the Byzantine scholars were infinitely more meticulous than their counterparts in the west. That said, Petrarch (1304-1374 CE) is noted as one of the first Western commentators in medieval history to romanticize the ancient past, recalling the works of Roman philosophers and historians. He is referred to as the first notable historical figure to introduce Humanism to Medieval Europe and promoted the vast importance of ancient history and literature.

Other notables include: Leonardo Bruni (1370-1444 CE), an Italian humanist, historian and statesman who is recognized as the first modern historian. His scholarship produced the first tripartite view of European history as Antiquity, Middle Age and Modern. Future historians such as Christoph Cellarius (1638-1707 CE), a German classical scholar later popularized this three-section categorization of European history.

The period itself was also divided by historians into three components: Early, High and Late Middle Ages. Early chroniclers such as Gregory, bishop of Tours (538-594 CE), penned numerous books including his most famous work, *Historia Francorum* (History of the Franks) in 591 CE. In it, he extols the great triumph of this era, which is the spread of Christianity in early France. Venerable Bede (672-735 CE), an English monk, accomplished similarly in England through his work *Historia Ecclesiastica Gentis Anglorum*, (Ecclesiastical History of the English People), in 731 CE. This book is not only a history of the Christian faith in England, but includes a history of Medieval England.

Modern era historians include Marc Léopold Benjamin Bloch (1886-1944 CE), a French historian and founding member of the Annales School of French social history. He is known for his studies in the field of medieval history and wrote extensively on Medieval France. In medieval studies, he is most noted for his book, *The Royal Touch: Monarchy and Miracles in France and England* (1924). In it, he studies the medieval superstition of the 'royal touch' and how kings used it for propaganda. Also, Johan Huizinga (1872-1945 CE), a Dutch historian and a founder of modern cultural history. His most famous work is *The Autumn of the Middle Ages*, 1919. Steven Runciman (1903-2000 CE), an English historian known for his three-volume work, A *History of the Crusades* (1951-1954 CE). This series has had a reflective impact on common notions of the Crusades, depicting the Crusaders in a bad light and the Muslims more positively.

2. Western Europe After Rome

As the Western Roman Empire receded after 500 CE, European civilization sustained multiple Germanic invasions ('barbarians' as viewed by the Romans) from its Northeastern borders, along with the evacuation of Roman authority throughout the West. The Western Roman Empire collapsed under the weight of its ongoing internal and external troubles. In this confluence of events, European cultures and what remained of local authorities mingled with the influx of Germanic peoples, while maintaining a vestige of their Roman heritage along with the acceptance of the new Christian religion. Throughout the Middle Ages and beyond, the community-rooted principles of barbarian law vied for authority with the state-rooted principles of Roman law. It is in the intersection between Germanic barbarian law and Roman law where we see the development of key principles and the established order that determined these customs and practices. The effect it had on various social groups led to the establishment of a new European code of law.

This new code was an amalgam of then current Germanic customs and traditions, and the legacies of Roman and Christian church cultures, which initiated the beginnings of a new legal structure that survives to modern times. However, as important as law was to the burgeoning Europeans during the Middle Ages, it was warfare that established their territories, cultures, economies and political structures. One cannot look at the Medieval Period without considering the effects of warfare, Christianity, Germanic influences, the contributions of the Byzantine Empire, the feudal system and the upheaval of the Black Plague.

Preceding the evolution of Western Europe after the decline of Rome, the Byzantine Empire (located in Eastern Europe in what is modern Greece and Turkey) is where Roman traditions were safeguarded. It is from Ancient Roman society that the Byzantine Empire would initially inherit its civilization and identity. The Byzantines considered themselves fully Roman even though they were located within the Hellenic and Greek worlds.

At the same time, while Western Europe was struggling with the collapse of the Western Roman Empire, Byzantium thrived. The 'Eastern Roman Empire', as they saw themselves, continued their great inheritance of what was the Roman Empire. The fledgling Western European cultures developed their own society independent from Byzantium.

It was through the establishment of Western powers, including the Franks (France), Germans and the burgeoning wealth of the Italian city-states such as Venice and Genoa that enabled the West to again flourish after Rome. Due to the Byzantines' efforts, the Justinian Legal Code and the Roman classics, science, math and politics were preserved. Law scholars refreshed its application in the West, most notably at the law school in Bologna, Italy, Europe's first university. The Roman classics, science, math and politics were revived by humanists like Petrarch, Leonardo Bruni, Erasmus, Nicholas of Cusa and many others.

Looking at the Western European timeline, in Gaul (France), the Carolingians - through victories in battle, tactical intermarriage and placement within the Merovingian court - were able, by the late 600s and early 700s, to usurp power from the Merovingians. A historically important Carolingian descendant is Charles Martel (714-741 CE) who is credited with repulsing Arab incursions into France at the Battles of Tours and Poitiers in 732 CE. Martel's military accomplishments extended Frankish authority and territory. The heirs to Martel were powerful nobles who held the position of Mayor of the Palace in the Merovingian court. This title gave the Carolingians complete control over the Frankish kings' household and secured their role in wielding the actual monarchical authority instead of the Merovingian kings themselves.

Martel's son and heir Pepin the Short (714-768 CE) finally did away with the pretense and appealed to Pope Zacharius (reigned 741-752 CE) in 751 CE that he was, in fact, the king and not the Merovingian king. The Church supported this appeal and crowned Pepin king making the Carolingians the new Frankish monarchy. Through this new alliance with the Church, the Carolingians consolidated power and authority in Frankish territories.

It was in this newly consolidated period that Pepin's son and heir Charles I (Charlemagne, reigned 768-814 CE) assumed kingship over the Franks as the first Holy Roman Emperor. Building on the successes of his forbearers, Charlemagne embodied the role of warrior-king. In 774 CE, continuing Carolingian good fortune of collaborating with the Church, Charlemagne vanquished the Lombards of Northern Italy who were long-time adversaries of the Papacy. This expanded Frankish territories into Northern Italy and provided the Papacy with territories in Central Italy, further solidifying their bond. Previously, the weakened Byzantines were unsuccessful in protecting the Papacy from the Lombards. This action shifted Papal allegiance away from the Eastern Empire to the Western Frankish monarchy. This shift in alliance had monumental historical consequences. The Papacy aligned with Western powers, providing significant recognition to Western civil authority and diminishing the hegemony of the Byzantines, which had been in place for over four centuries. Charlemagne was coronated by Pope Leo III (reigned 795-816 CE) as the Western Roman Emperor in 800 CE, much to the chagrin of the Byzantines. This act, in combination with Charlemagne's military victories consolidating mainland Europe, made him the undisputed leader of Western 'Christendom'. Charlemagne recollected Roman times by building a cathedral at Aachen (located between modern Belgium and Germany near Cologne), which was likened to the Hagia Sophia in Constantinople.

While such progress was an enormous beginning to the formation of Western Europe, Charlemagne's empire was unable to improve its economic status. Population centers continued to be remote and disconnected, keeping industry and trade low. Nobles maintained control of local territories and were sworn to uphold Charlemagne's laws and rule, but they continued to rest on the recognition and reward system which remained frail. As a result, violence, crime and kin civil strife continued under his rule. The feudal state where peasants were bound to local strongmen remained and even burgeoned throughout Charlemagne's reign. The ongoing practice of dividing inheritance among children would eventually undermine Charlemagne's empire as well. While Charlemagne's strong reputation was enough to keep the loose empire together, his successors could not, and so the short-lived Western Empire would dissolve after Charlemagne.

Later, Holy Roman Emperor Frederick I Barbarossa (1122-1190 CE) assumed his empire as the Justinian legal Code was resurging in Western Europe. It helped Frederick to effectively manage the Western Roman Empire in the same organized manner much as the Romans and Byzantines had done. Like Justinian, Frederick used the Code to justify his lordship over Germany and Italy and legitimize monarchical sovereignty as different from and superior to papal authority.

Prior to Frederick, the Papacy prevailed against the Western kings in what is known as the Investiture Controversy. The Papacy fought with Western monarchies over the right to invest bishops and abbots throughout the 11th and 12th centuries. Western leaders claimed the 'divine right of kings' over papal authority. Papal authority, however, prevailed. The Church's success resulting from the Investiture Controversy, much like the Justinian Code did in Byzantium, consolidated Western powers under the banner of Christianity. The Justinian Code balanced this power by providing a legal framework for Frederick's imperial aspirations, thus giving Frederick the concept that he was the legitimate inheritor and successor to Imperial Rome like Charlemagne did before him. This fracture, however, set up the groundwork for future discord between the church and popular sentiments.

Frederick's resurrection of the Justinian Code helped improve feudalism, the prevailing European political system. Feudalism was a remnant from the collapse of the Western Roman Empire and dominated Medieval Europe for over five-hundred years. In the vacuum of Roman power, enclaves of populations that fled from cities to the hinterlands to get away from the lawlessness and conflict of Rome's collapse gathered under strongmen who traded their protection for goods and services. This was the regressive feudal system. So while the sovereigns of Europe continued to bolster their legitimacy using the legacies of Roman law, the masses abided under the system of feudal law. Feudal law was essentially a gathering of civil laws and military practices, taken from Germanic customs and cannon law (church law) practiced in Europe, whereby strong and prosperous land owners managed property and labor in service to greater lords. The land owners, usually legally recognized, were considered nobles who carried a specific level of authority, title and rank for services rendered. In turn, nobles had vassals who took oaths of fealty and peasants that managed their property and land, both in service to the nobles. These reciprocal relationships prevailed in Europe from approximately 900-1800 CE in various forms. After 1500 CE, feudalism waned considerably. Under the feudal system, the sword protected European populations from certain death in the absence of the Roman legal and military systems.

The adoption of Christianity also had considerable influence over Germanic traditions entrenched in Western Europe after the Roman collapse. The Christian church operated under canon law. Canon law is a gathering of rubrics that are based in Old and New Testament scripture descended from the early Church. Canon law continued to develop throughout European history, adopting components of Roman law and later Germanic law. The traditions of the 'Peace of God' and 'Truce of God' propagated by the Church cooperated with the attitudes found in Germanic customs. The Peace and Truce of God were an attempt by the Church to curtail the bitter and bloody rivalries between Europe's noble families and were later encoded into canon law and replaced *Pax Romana*. These traditions also helped the Church to indoctrinate

Christian ethics into Germanic culture. Church involvement in the pacification was also part of its efforts to convert Germanic society from its pagan traditions. These religious dispositions were considered dangerous to the Christian church's mission and, therefore, much was done to Christianize the Germanic tribes.

Christianity was popular; therefore it was greatly valued by the German kings as a unifying force. As a result, in a relatively short period Christianity became the religion of Europe. Far from simply adopting Roman law, the Germanic social system absorbed the cultural heritage not only of the Romans, who they had become familiar with prior to the collapse of Rome's power in Europe, but also assimilated Canon law, which was the code of the Christian Church.

Many Germanic traditions and customs remained, but they were ultimately changed by the many new influences of European civilization. Germanic law prevailed during the period right after Rome's breakdown until Roman law was reconstituted in the later Middle Ages. As the European economy improved and the population resurged after the Black Death, its legal system again required updating. Archaic feudal and agrarian society gave way to a more sophisticated and urbanized way of life. Law and dispute settlements needed modernization. France led the way by appointing only those with law degrees to its highest court, but remained challenged by its application, because the populace still regarded Germanic customs as an important part of the legal system. Kings needed to maintain order but often judged on the side of the written Roman law as taught by universities. Feudalism in England was dramatically altered after the adoption of the *Magna Carta* in 1215 CE, when nobles sought additional rights from the king, especially regarding land ownership.

Three main foundations of law supported the stability of Western civilization during the turbulent years after the collapse of the Western Roman Empire: Roman law as conveyed by the Byzantine Empire through Justinian's Code (which was lost after the 6th century and rediscovered in the 11th), Germanic law (which was later a hybrid of Roman and Gothic tribal customs) and canon law of the Christian Church (which carried its traditions from Biblical teachings and Roman law).

Over the 1,000 year period from 500 to 1500 CE, Europe's legal system progressed from its Roman roots, assimilated Germanic traditions and incorporated Christian morality and ethics. Along with the social upheavals brought about by the Black Death and the empowerment of Europe's bourgeoisie class, power-sharing began to move from monarchs to wider popular consent, as seen in the establishment of the jury system and early forms of parliament.

3. Blood on the Sword

Warfare in feudal Europe was not simply a history of cavalry battles, mounted knights and castle sieges as characterized by popular romanticism, which are indeed remarkable; but was more importantly an essential political tool resulting from dramatic social, economic and cultural changes that deeply affected emergent Western Europe after the fall of the Western Roman Empire. By this time, Medieval Europe's population grew, resulting from advancements in farming technology, the cessation of barbarian raids and the spread of Christianity. The earthly establishment of Christendom had the effect of consolidating disparate tribes under one belief system and one spiritual leader in the ascending Roman Papacy. Disputes over spiritual and temporal primacy occupied the Catholic Church and European civil authorities for centuries prior, but by the 12th century the dispute was addressed and the unity that followed strengthened Western Europe. Additionally, Western Europe continued its separation from Byzantium, providing it with an encouraged self-identity. Western Europe expanded its borders by conquests into what were previously Muslim territory in Spain, Byzantine territory in Italy and Sicily, and Slavic territory in the Balkans and Eastern Europe. A major component of these conquests and expansions included the period of the Crusades.

Western Europe's sovereigns, after the collapse of Charlemagne's Holy Roman Empire, became an arrangement of decentralized civil authorities that relied on the feudal system for political, social and economic organization. Feudal law was essentially a gathering of Roman civil laws and military practices taken from Germanic customs and cannon law (church law) practiced in Medieval Europe, whereby strong and prosperous land owners managed fighters, property and labor in service to country and the baron. The land owners (nobles), usually legally recognized by the king or sovereigns themselves, were considered nobles who carried a specific level of authority, title or rank. In turn, nobles had vassals (knights) who took oaths of fealty and peasants who managed the nobles' property and land, both in service to the noble. These were called fiefs, a word derived from the Latin term *fuedum*.

As such, feudal society relied on strength-of-arms for the protection and expansion of their population, economy and civil authority. Medieval aristocrats were a military-class. From childhood, males were trained for warfare with skills of horse-mounted combat and to exhibit strong cultural attitudes of gallantry. As mentioned, the aristocracy was classified into two tiers: nobles and knights. Together they developed a common code of behavior called, 'chivalry' (from *cheval*, the French word for horse). Knights in service to nobles were prepared for war, the protection of the nobles' fiefs and local churches from invaders, and they enforced law and order.

Medieval warfare included the development of advanced fortifications around the manorial estates which were initially wooden structures then later stone castles. The general mainstay of feudal warfare consisted of castle sieges, private conflicts between and among competing nobles and the nobles' armies invading enemy lands and villages. Knights were strong and well protected through use of armor and battle horses. The horse saddle stirrup was a significant technological advancement that arrived in Europe during the Middle Ages and that expedited the success of mounted conflict. Mounted knights were deadly and the most advanced combat delivery system of that period. They were a very formidable power at the command of the civil authorities. Part of the mounted knights' arsenals included pole-arms (lance, spear, javelin), which were employed at a full gallop against enemies, blades (swords), ranged weapons (bow, crossbow), axes, maces and the like. Once dismounted, the knight could employ any number of weapons for hand-to-hand fighting. Knights were armed by their nobles because fighting equipment was expensive, but at times knights were also required to supply their own materials. Nobles displayed their loyalty by providing knights with armor, weapons lands and titles of their own. The distinction between nobles and knights became less clear over time as fortunes rose and fell and knights became more enriched.

Knights led the nobles' armies which varied organizationally. In the Early Middle Ages, mounted knights led lieutenants, who assisted the knights and were of higher quality combat skills than regulars or militia. Others would be gathered from local militia or citizens having little fighting experience. By the High Middle Ages, when sovereigns were more powerful and political systems more structured, recruiting of young men took place out of the land-owning - but not noble - classes. Paid mercenaries were also used.

During peacetime, nobles hosted tournaments for their knights to compete in mock warfare and to enact a rudimentary form of justice where petty squabbles were resolved or ransoms were paid for important, captured enemies. Tournaments were a fantastic spectacle for the common people and all kinds of services and diversions were available, much like what the Roman poet Juvenal referred to as the entertainment of bread and circuses of ancient Rome, or modern-day professional sports events. However, military prowess in Medieval Europe was a serious business and it prepared men for actual warfare, who were in constant demand because this also contributed to a high mortality rate among male warriors.

Given the state of affairs outside of burgeoning Medieval Europe, aside from competing nobles, interlopers and enemies often relied on sacking or plundering for sustenance. Men-at-arms were the primary defense against such attacks. Initially, nobles fortified their manor estates with sturdy homes that were defended by their knights, but as warfare became more complex, greater structures were called for to defend against elaborate sieges. Castles, as a central part of a noble's land holdings, grew rapidly throughout the High Middle Ages. Castles neutralized open-field cavalry attacks and allowed the nobles to employ archers to slow the onslaughts of attackers, while precious family and property were safeguarded. As castle impenetrability increased, so did the employment of technologies used for castle sieges, such as siege towers and catapults. Measures and counter-measures of siege warfare continued to advance throughout this period as more intricate technologies and strategies were discovered or employed. Castle architecture became more sophisticated as well. From simple four-walled structures, castles grew into magnificent compounds which could encompass entire towns. Much more time could be spent analyzing castle development during this period, as evidenced by the many castles found throughout Europe standing today.

Feudal warfare was an essential part of Western Europe's political and social system. Europe's political and social culture matured out of indigenous populations who were in decline after the fall of the Western Roman Empire, absorbing a massive influx of barbarian tribes. This was the root for modern European nations such as France, England and Poland. Not only did these customs and practices establish monarchies and sovereign states, but contributed to strong economic structures and legal systems that supported organized civilization.

Feudal warfare fueled a significant growth phase of Medieval Europe between the 1100s and the 1300s. The feudal state was a dynamic system that was immensely useful in maintaining an ordered society as Europe expanded through improved food supplies, housing, clothing and social opportunities. Improved farming increased revenues and provided greater mobility for peasants and nobles alike. Feudal warfare maintained a political structure and balance of power among nobles, tribes and nations. The warrior-class of Europe's Middle Ages was the foundation for their expansion, security, leadership and stability.

4. The Black Plague and Its Aftermath

The period between 1347 CE and 1350 CE is regarded by most historians as the years in which the Black Death reached its devastating zenith in Europe. It spread to nearly all European countries that were routine trading partners. Where trade from other European countries was limited, such lands were less affected by the Plague. Consequently, countries such as Poland and other remote locations were primarily exempted from the outbreak. As a side note, the term "The Black Death" is a modern term used for this epidemic. While the Great Plague struck often throughout the late 14th and 15th centuries, the years 1347-1350 CE were the hardest hit, given that no immunities to the disease were yet developed.

The disease was introduced into Europe from its southern seaports in Sicily and France, arriving from Asian trading partners. Keeping with prevailing theories, rodents on trading ships carried fleas that were infected with the Plague. Due to the living conditions found in Europe at that time, where cities were generally unsanitary, people were undernourished and cohabitated with animals, it was a fertile environment for the rapid spread of the pestilence. Those practiced in physic and healing were completely powerless against its ravages, causing great panic and fear.

Given the large scale death and depopulation caused by the Plague, its impact on Europe's political, social and economic systems was colossal. The harvesting of grain and wool rapidly declined as the labor market significantly contracted. Farmlands not abandoned increased the need for labor to the benefit of those who survived. Rents on farmland dropped due the increase in availability. This led to a growing wealthy class of prosperous farmers who gobbled up available lands, increasing their market share. Wages increased considerably for laborers due to the vacancies. Combined, this had the effect of decreasing serfdom as laborers' lot improved. People rebelled against the social-economic system forever after sparking a spirit of revolt against the crushing system of serfdom. Nobles had to contend with this popular sentiment from that point forward, leading to later improvements in the management of the nobility's estates.

Prices for food also fell while labor costs increased. To offset this impact, landowners rented some of their fields to peasants, which also improved their working conditions. Trade was also interrupted because the underpinnings of the market collapsed: contracts, trade partnerships and production. Urban centers experienced an economic depression. This caused wealthy leaders of trade guilds to become more restrictive in order to retain their power.

European aristocracy was also affected greatly by the Plague. Family heredities ended when nobles died. While the decline of serfdom reduced the local nobility's influence, royal monarchies became more powerful as the gap widened between the wealthy and lower classes of nobles. Monarchs sought to consolidate power as the aristocracy was reduced. Governments were caught off guard and the people lost confidence in leadership. In some instances Jews were blamed and persecution ensued, killing some Jewish communities. Local governments were ravaged, leading to chaos during the Plague years. It took some time to recover after the initial shock of the Plague, but Europe's economic and political structures would be forever changed resulting from its epic effects.

5. The Church and Reform

Central to the Middle Ages were the Mass and Purgatory as pillars of the Church. Luther noted that the Bible's New Testament only referenced heaven and hell. Church thinkers had developed the concept of Purgatory as a middle space between heaven and hell against what Luther believed to be strict Biblical context. Moreover, the Church literally capitalized on this condition by selling indulgences that would mitigate time spent in Purgatory, speeding the faithful to heaven. Luther's call for reform and resistance to the Church set the stage for seismic shifts in European culture.

The Reformation and Counter-Reformation were the culmination of the changes that occurred through the Middle Ages. Much of it built upon the blood of the sword. It was a revolt not only against Church practices, but against the establishment of cultural identities in Western Europe: the North Protestant and the South Catholic. The Counter-reformation re-entrenched the Catholic Church in its teachings and reform as well, which bolstered its holding in Southern Europe, mainly in Spain, France, and Italy.

Often overlooked in European history is the German Peasants; War where mass violence erupted across Germany. Relatively unknown in popular history, this war was Europe's most massive and widespread popular uprising before the 1789 French Revolution. While the revolts failed under the crushing check of the aristocracy, social change had already taken hold. The spark of reform that Luther ignited further enabled the populace to question the old hierarchical system. What followed was a series of widespread and devastating wars from the early 1500s through the late 1600s that included the Eighty Years' War (1568-1648 CE), the French Wars of Religion (1562-1598 CE), the Thirty Years' War (1618-1648 CE), the Wars of the Three Kingdoms (1639-

1651 CE), and several others that redefined Europe's geopolitical boundaries.

Europe was divided along religious/geographic lines. Generally, Roman Catholic territories were located in the southwest and Lutheran/Reformed territories were located in the northeast, with pockets of other sects in between. It wasn't until the Peace of Westphalia (1648 CE) that the religious wars of Europe ended. Europe's sovereign territories took shape, ending the dream of the Holy Roman Empire where Europe would serve one rule for all of Christendom. After 1648 CE, there was no prospect that this foundation institution of the Medieval Western Christendom was ever going to become a coherent, bureaucratic and centralized state. Europe's map today looks nearly as it did those many centuries ago. In this we can see why the sword had the most significant impact on modern European history. In fact, it was the warrior-class of Europe's Middle Ages that was the foundation for their expansion, security, leadership and stability. The resurgence of Roman law and great inventions such as the printing press and the book cannot be overstated; however, while these artifacts were the spark under the flame of Renaissance ideas that emerged during the late Middle Ages, it was the sword that brought massive change to Europe, which remains today.

6. Conclusion

Given all of these considerations of the Middle Ages, on one hand, Western Europe had the transmission of law from the Romans through the Byzantines, the tribal laws of the Germanic tribes, the reintroduction of the Roman Classics, the coalescence of one religious system and the invention of the printing press. On the other hand, Western Europe had the Black Plague, the feudal warrior state, the conquests of disparate tribes, the repulsion of Arabs from Europe and the papal conflicts. Ironically, it was the mass-produced book from the printing press that sparked the wars of religion, mainly in Germany and Northern Europe that divided the Church, which reigned for a millennium after Rome's decline. Far from being 'Dark Ages', it was during this period that the blood of the sword laid the foundation of the periods to come: the Reformation, Renaissance, Enlightenment and Scientific Age.

Background

Societal 'laws' that developed from the early Middle Ages took their root in diverse sources. As the Western Roman Empire receded after 500 CE, European civilization sustained multiple Germanic invasions ('barbarians' as viewed by the Romans) from its Northeastern borders along with the evacuation of Roman authority throughout the West. The Western Roman Empire collapsed under the weight of its ongoing internal and external troubles. In this confluence of events, European cultures and what remained of local authorities mingled with the influx of Germanic peoples while maintaining a vestige of their Roman heritage along with the acceptance of the new Christian religion. Bennett observes, "...throughout the Middle Ages and beyond, the community-rooted principles of barbarian law vied for authority with the state-rooted principles of Roman law."[43] It is in the intersection between Germanic barbarian law and Roman law where we see the development of key principles and the established order that determined these customs and practices. The effect it had on various social groups led to the establishment of a new European code of law. This new code was an amalgam of then current Germanic customs and traditions, the legacies of Roman and Christian church cultures, which initiated the beginnings of a new legal structure that survives to modern times.

Preceding the newly established Germanic peoples, the Byzantine Empire (located in Eastern Europe in what is today modern-day Greece and Turkey) retained what it could of the Roman tradition. It is from Ancient Roman society that the Byzantine Empire would initially inherit its civilization and identity. The Byzantines considered themselves fully Roman, even though it was located within the Hellenic and Greek worlds. Constantine I (Roman Emperor, 272-337 CE) moved the capital of the Empire from Rome to Byzantium - a Greek colony that was later renamed Constantinople - in 324 CE. Later, between 529 CE and 535 CE, Justinian I (Byzantine Emperor, 482-565 CE) commissioned a distinguished panel of jurists presided over by Tribonian (485-542 CE)

---

[43] Judith Bennett , *Medieval Europe: A Short History*, (McGraw-Hill Higher Education: 11th Edition, 2011), 23.

to regulate Roman law into a systematic, organized and useable format: The *Corpus Juris Civilis* (*Justinian Code*). Prior to this, Roman law was a disparate accumulation of established laws, judicial outcomes and case precedence from over 1,000 years of practice within the Roman civilization. This was not the first time a Byzantine emperor had undertaken such a monumental task, but Justinian's became the quintessential legal standard for centuries to come.

At the same time, while Western Europe was struggling with the collapse of the Western Roman Empire, Byzantium thrived. The 'Eastern Roman Empire' - as they saw themselves - continued their great inheritance of what was the Roman Empire. One of the major factors that made Justinian's Code different than the Roman law is that it also incorporated the Christian worldview. Christian morality, philosophy and ethics were a hefty consideration for Justinian and Byzantine society as they interpreted and applied Roman law. What is also clear is that Justinian's Code was not simply an organizational improvement over prior Roman law, but it was updated to include existing Hellenistic culture and customs found throughout Byzantium. The Justinian Code saw later updates by subsequent Emperors until Byzantium's demise at the hands of the Ottomans in 1453 CE. By this time, the fledgling Western European cultures developed their own legal code independent from Byzantium.

George Ostrogorsky observes that, "In the Byzantine Empire, Roman law remained the basis of legal development throughout its history, and Justinian's *Corpus* was the starting point for all future work in this field."[44] After the collapse of the Western Roman Empire it was the Byzantines who preserved the classical Greek and Roman legal structures for future generations. Roman law diminished in the West due to the vacuum of political power and leadership, but was later revived through its use by the Holy Roman Emperor Frederick I Barbarossa (1122-1190 CE).

It was through the establishment of Western powers including the Franks, Germans and the burgeoning wealth of the Italian city-states such as Venice and Genoa that enabled the West to again embrace the

---

[44] George Ostrogorsky, *History of the Byzantine State*, (New Brunswick, NJ: Rutgers University Press, 1969), 77.

study of classical law. Due to the Byzantines' efforts, the Justinian Code was preserved. Law scholars refreshed its application in the West, most notably at the law school in Bologna, Italy, Europe's first university.

Frederick I assumed his empire as the Justinian Code was resurging in Western Europe. It helped Frederick to effectively manage the Western Roman Empire in the same organized manner much as the Romans and Byzantines had done. Like Justinian, Frederick used the Code to justify his lordship over Germany and Italy and legitimize monarchical sovereignty as different from and superior to papal authority. Prior to Frederick, the Papacy prevailed against the Western kings in what is known as the Investiture Controversy. The Papacy fought with Western monarchies over the right to invest bishops and abbots throughout the 11th and 12th centuries. Western leaders claimed the 'divine right of kings' over papal authority. Papal authority, however, prevailed. The church's success resulting from the Investiture Controversy, much like the Justinian Code did in Byzantium, consolidated Western powers under the banner of Christianity. The Justinian Code balanced this power by providing a legal framework for Frederick's imperial aspirations, thus giving Frederick the concept that he was the legitimate inheritor and successor to Imperial Rome, like Charlemagne (748-814 CE) did before him.

Frederick's resurrection of the Justinian Code helped improve feudalism, the prevailing European political system. Feudalism was a remnant from the collapse of the Western Roman Empire and dominated Medieval Europe for over five-hundred years. So while the sovereigns of Europe continued to bolster their legitimacy using the legacies of Roman law, the masses abided under the system of feudal law. Feudal law was essentially a gathering of civil laws and military practices taken from Germanic customs, and cannon law (church law) practiced in Europe, whereby strong and prosperous land owners managed property and labor in service to greater lords. The land owners, usually legally recognized were considered nobles who carried a specific level of authority, title and rank for services rendered. In turn, nobles had vassals who took oaths of fealty and peasants that managed their property and land, both in service to the nobles. These were called fiefs, a word derived from the Latin term *fuedum*. Stuart M. Madden relays that, "...the law codes of the

101

Lombards, the Burgundians, and the Salian Franks provided a civilizing legal bridge between the fall of the Western Empire and the more Westernized law codes that would follow in the later Middle Ages."[45] These reciprocal relationships prevailed in Europe from approximately 900-1800 CE in various forms. After 1500 CE, feudalism waned considerably.

So, while the Byzantine Empire carried on the traditions of Rome in the East, the West was confronted with a very different reality. Stepping back to the period prior to Charlemagne (reigned 800-828 CE) the Germanic tribes' (known to the Romans as barbarians) infiltration of the Western Roman Empire had significant cultural and political influences. Barbarians were different than the Romans in that they were agrarian pastoralists and hierarchical warrior clans. Bennett states, "...they [barbarians]...organized their societies on four foundations: kindred, war-bands, law codes and eventually ethnicity, as expressed through kingship."[46] In a strange twist of fate, the introduction of these practices helped soften the fall of the Western Roman Empire.

Modern historians struggle to piece together a specific understanding of how barbarian law (Germanic law), known as *leges barbarorum*, was applied. Over the centuries after Rome's fall, specific Germanic laws were implemented by the following tribes from the late 5th century through the 9th century: Visigoths, Burgundians, Franks, Alamanni, Lombards, Visigoths, Bavarians, Frisians, Saxons and Thuringians. While Germanic law was often independent of Roman law, there are still many other examples where Germanic law borrowed from Roman law especially those preserved by the Byzantines. The Visigoths were the first of the Germanic tribes to produce a set of laws in 480 and included many referenced from the Byzantine Empire. Prior to this and to Justinian's Code, in 429 Theodosius II (401-450 CE), the Byzantine emperor attempted to codify Roman law into what is known as the *Codex Theodosianus*. Theodosius' efforts were the first (since the *Law of the Twelve Tables* of Republican Rome) to collect, organize and publish

---

[45] M. Stuart Madden, *Paths of Western Law after Justinian*, (Widener Law Journal, 22, 3: 2013), 758.
[46] Judith Bennett, *Medieval Europe: A Short History*, (McGraw-Hill Higher Education, 11th Edition: 2011), 40.

existing laws. The Visigoths borrowed from the *Codex* and combined it with their own legal customs.

Many documents exist, especially those of the later Franks under the Carolingian dynasty, but their direct link to a legal code is not always clear. These were an attempt to update the ancient Germanic laws. Many believe they were developed from local meetings and agreements among the nobility, not always decrees by the Germanic kings. The chronicles show that kings and their councils played a major role in administering justice, but their laws were not recorded as a precise codified system, and not in all instances promulgated by kings. Faulkner asserts that, "They [the documents] suggest that the *leges* were used broadly, practically and flexibly in disputes, and were not seen as official, royally endorsed law."[47] These new laws attempted to modernize the *leges barbarorum*. By the time the Carolingians encoded the barbarian customs into a more formal legal code in the 9th century, the *leges barbarorum* were already over 300 years old. In Charlemagne's effort to codify barbarian laws inclusive of Roman laws and church laws, his court meticulously pieced together the various components that contributed to modernizing Carolingian law. The Frank's focus on establishing clan identity can be seen in their efforts. The existing texts indicate that during the early French kingdom and Holy Roman Empire, under the Carolingians, that the Franks made an effort to directly enshrine in a legal codex the specific laws of the Roman Empire, but completion of this project was not completed until Frederick I four centuries later.

Under the *leges barbarorum* or Germanic law, leaders were chosen as magistrates (usually kings) who made judgments in matters of conflict, disputes or on anything that today we would consider legal matters. This gave magistrates a wide range of subjective treatment on the issues presented before them. Much of what we know about Germanic law comes from what was memorialized by later generations of the Franks and Germans.

As previously stated, Germanic law was more oral than a codified set of written laws, as in Roman law. The Germanic tribes brought a unique set of customs and traditions to what were previously the Western

---

[47] Thomas Faulkner, *Carolingian Kings and the Leges Barbarorum*, (Historical Research, 86, 233: August 2013), 443.

Roman provinces. It is often erroneously thought that Germanic tribes were more heavily influenced by Rome. Insight is gained by looking at a then contemporary work by a Roman historian, Tacitus (56-117 CE). Tacitus' *Germania* is a controversial historical work that was lost through the Middle Ages, but was rediscovered in 1425 CE. As a side note, the use of the word 'German' fell out of use until revived by Tacitus' work, when the term was rediscovered. It was deemed controversial because recent studies have attributed the actions of German nationalism in the 20th century to its warlike descriptions of the Germanic peoples including their mythological origins. Despite this, his work has contributed an enlightening perspective on Germanic identity in the shadow of Europe's Roman heritage and legal legacy. According to Leitch, "The discovery of Tacitus' *Germania* linked humanist exploration of the past...to a search for the origins of the Germans themselves···Tacitus' work forced a reconsideration of the truth of a genealogy in which Germans were imagined as reincarnated Romans, and put such local legends into historical perspective."[48] Further, Leitch concludes, "With the evidence supplied by Tacitus, humanists...nationalized the conceptual wild man and turned him into a German citizen nonpareil."[49] This observation helps to understand how unique Germanic customs were often independent of Roman influences.

Conversely, much like the Romans, family or kinship was an important basis for their social organization. People were often set within a certain class or social status: chieftains (kings), nobles, warriors and peasants. Higher clergy were later introduced into the nobility class when Christianity took root within the Germanic culture. Unlike Roman law, Germanic law was set on principles of reparations rather than penalties. If a custom was broken or an offense committed, reparations were assessed by the magistrates and had to be paid to the offended party or parties relative to their social status. Capital punishment was reserved for extreme cases only. Capital crimes may have included treason to the chieftain, desertion or mutiny in the war band, and sexual crimes. Reparations were called *wergild* in the Germanic language. *Wergild* was

---

[48] Stephanie Leitch, *The Wild Man, Charlemagne and the German Body*, (Art History, 31, 3: June 2008), 285.
[49] Ibid. Leitch, 286.

established as a sum of money that could be multiplied relative to the offense and further increased when considering to whom it was committed. A higher ranking social status meant a higher *wergild* was to be paid.

Germanic kings were viewed as divinely appointed. Their strength and leadership were seen as God-given qualities that were crucial for tribal survival. Law was viewed as a necessity when problems cropped up, but it was the king's duty to deliver justice, not punishment. It was believed that legal adjudication was to be tempered by mercy and patriarchal care. Traditional and tribal practices were the basis for administering justice and were aligned with what the tribes believed to be normative social standards. In the beginning, Germanic kings applied their laws to their own people and judged people of the Roman territories they occupied with Roman law. Eventually, the two were blended together.

Germanic law and the ancient Roman *mos maiorum* were similar in that they were unwritten, but held moral sway over their communities. To compare, Ancient Rome was a deeply moral and principled culture steeped in religion and based upon a solid foundation of social customs and traditions like the Germanic tribes. In its seminal period, before Rome established itself as a firm polity, these social customs were unwritten, but deeply rooted in their tribal norms, mores and folkways. These customs are known in Latin as the *mos maiorum* or ancestral customs, literally 'custom (way) of our ancestors (elders)'. The *mos maiorum* provided the moral inspiration that propelled the disparate Latin tribes to gather and flourish into the Roman civilization which eventually developed Roman law. Roman law was transcribed, edited throughout Rome's history and then later expanded by the Byzantine Empire to include Christian morality. The Germanic tribes respected Roman law and established its own unwritten customs into a blend of Germanic, church and Roman laws.

Pointed out earlier, Germanic law preferred to settle differences through compensation rather than through blood feuds or vengeance and are a departure from Roman law. This had the effect of redirecting Medieval European culture toward a more peaceful carriage of justice. Madden observes, "These changes in Germanic law gave an increased likelihood of even-handed administration of justice, and provided also a monetized incentive for the family of a victim to forego mayhem in resolving disputes."[50] These changes were welcomed as European society transformed after the Germanic invasions from war bands to a new culture based on agriculture instead of conquest.

The adoption of Christianity also had considerable influence over Germanic traditions. The Christian church operated under canon law. Canon law is a gathering of rubrics that are based in Old and New Testament Scripture descended from the early Church. Canon law continued to develop throughout European history, also adopting components of Roman law and later Germanic law. The traditions of the 'Peace of God' and 'Truce of God' propagated by the Church cooperated with the attitudes found in Germanic customs. The Peace and Truce of God were an attempt by the Church to curtail the bitter and bloody rivalries between Europe's noble families and were later encoded into Canon law. These traditions also helped the Church to indoctrinate Christian ethics into Germanic culture. In this regard, Bisson asserts, "It has often been suggested that the religious peace was secularized...yet it may prove instructive to think of pacification as a persistently clerical - and cultural - influence on the remodeling of justice...." Church involvement in the pacification was also part of its efforts to convert Germanic society from its pagan traditions. Regarding this, Metzner notes that, "The religion of the ancient Germanic peoples was animistic, pagan, and panentheistic...Animistic means all natural phenomena were seen as animated by vital force and sentience... Pagan means it was the religion of country-dwellers...Panentheistic means the belief that all of creation is sacred...."[51] These religious dispositions were considered dangerous to the Christian Church's mission and, therefore, much was done to Christianize the Germanic tribes. Christianity was popular; therefore it was greatly valued by the German kings as a unifying force. As a result, in a relatively short period Christianity became the religion of Europe. Far from simply adopting Roman law, the Germanic social system absorbed the cultural heritage not only of the Romans who they

---

[50] M. Stuart Madden, *Paths of Western Law After Justinian*, (Widener Law Journal, 22, 3: 2013), 758.
[51] Ralph Metzner, *Germanic Mythology and the Fate of Europe* (ReVision, 13, 1: Summer 1990), 17.

had become familiar with prior to the collapse of Rome's power in Europe, but also assimilated Canon law which was the code of the Christian church.

Many Germanic traditions and customs remained, but they were ultimately changed by the many new influences of European civilization. Germanic law prevailed during the period right after Rome's breakdown until Roman law was reconstituted in the later Middle Ages. As the European economy improved and the population resurged after the Black Death, its legal system again required updating. According to van Caenegem, "Around the twelfth century Europe embarked upon a new phase and made enormous progress in the economic, legal and cultural field. Archaic feudal and agrarian society gave way to a more sophisticated and urbanized way of life. Law and dispute settlements needed modernization."[52] France led the way by appointing only those with law degrees to its highest court, but remained challenged by its application because the populace still regarded Germanic customs as an important part of the legal system. Kings needed to maintain order but often judged on the side of the written Roman law as taught by universities. This was another way that customary law was blended with Roman law, furthering the hybridization of European law.

Van Caenegem further declares that the medieval legal system made two significant contributions to Western law: the jury and popular representation. He states, "Just as democratic as the jury, but this time rooted in medieval Roman law, is the notion that matters which concern the whole community ought to be decided by all its members."[53] In this, the foundations of early parliaments were laid. Kings who previously issues decrees or convened private councils had to contend with nobles demanding popular participation in government. This was coupled with the large scale death and depopulation caused by the Black Plague's colossal impact on Europe's political, social and economic systems. People rebelled against the social-economic system forever after sparking a spirit of revolt against the crushing system of serfdom. Nobles had to contend with this popular sentiment from that point

---

[52], R.C. van Caenegem *The Modernity of Medieval Law,* (Legal History Review, 68, 3: September 2000), 318.
[53] Ibid. Caenegem, 320.

forward, leading to later improvements in the management of the nobility's estates and the acceptance of popular involvement in government in the form of parliament.

England was not as principally influenced as the continental European states, because it had already developed its own legal standards by the time the Justinian Code was revived. England produced its own laws called *common law*. However, it must be noted that English law was likely shaped by Roman law in that its earliest lawgivers, such as Edward the Confessor (1005-1066 CE), who in his early years received much of his legal knowledge during his exile in continental Europe and conveyed such experiences to England when he became its ruler in 1042 CE.

Feudalism in England was dramatically altered after the adoption of the *Magna Carta* in 1215 CE, when nobles sought additional rights from the king especially regarding land ownership. By 1645 CE, England's Parliament effectively abolished feudalism and adopted many of the practices borrowed from the legacies of Roman law. Parallel to developments in continental Europe, English feudalism began to wane due to the obvious shortfalls in legal clarity under English Common law and European Feudal law.

With the advent of the Renaissance and the Age of Enlightenment, law principles again changed. By the end of the 17th century, the idea of natural rights permeated Enlightenment-age philosophy and found its way into the legal concepts of human rights: self-evident and inalienable rights of humanity that were not provided by any person, sovereign or legal system, but are universal and freely inherent in human existence. Later, popular revolutions in America and France would fuel even greater change to law practice. It is upon the foundations of Germanic law, Roman law and Canon law introduced into Medieval Europe at the end of the Western Roman Empire that helped preserve Europe's stability, enabling it to transform from a set of Roman provinces into what are later European states.

Three main foundations of law supported the stability of Western civilization during the turbulent years after the collapse of the Western Roman Empire: Roman law as conveyed by the Byzantine Empire through Justinian's Code (which was lost after the 6th century and rediscovered in the 11th), Germanic law (which was later a hybrid of Roman and Gothic tribal customs) and Canon law of the Christian Church (which carried its traditions from Biblical teachings and Roman law). Roman law waned during the Early Middle Ages, but remained influential even combining with Germanic law. The Germanic tribes, although in control of most of Western Europe, greatly respected Roman civilization and sought to emulate some of its major customs including its legal practices under Roman law.

Over the one-thousand year period from 500 CE to 1500 CE, Europe's legal system progressed from its Roman roots, assimilated Germanic traditions and incorporated Christian morality and ethics. Along with the social upheavals brought about by the Black Death and the empowerment of Europe's bourgeoisie class, power sharing began to move from monarchs to wider popular consent, as seen in the establishment of the jury system and early forms of parliament. Such progress would later coalesce into Western law in practice today. Western law, resulting from these foundations introduced concepts that are often the goals of many modern nations which include: limited and balanced governmental powers, civil and individual liberty, free economic markets and self-determination that empower citizens over governments.

Bennett, Judith. *Medieval Europe: A Short History*. McGraw-Hill Higher Education:11th Edition, (2011). 23.

Ostrogorsky, George. *History of the Byzantine State*. New Brunswick, NJ: Rutgers University Press, (1969). 77.

Madden, M. Stuart. *Paths of Western Law after Justinian*. Widener Law Journal: 22, 3 (2013). 758.

Bennett, Judith. *Medieval Europe: A Short History*. McGraw-Hill Higher Education: 11th Edition (2011). 40.

Faulkner, Thomas. *Carolingian Kings and the Leges Barbarorum*. Historical Research: 86, 233 (August 2013). 443.

Leitch, Stephanie. *The Wild Man, Charlemagne and the German Body*. Art History: 31, 3 (June 2008). 285.

Leitch, Stephanie. *The Wild Man, Charlemagne and the German Body*. Art History: 31, 3 (June 2008). 286.

Madden, M. Stuart. *Paths of Western Law After Justinian*. Widener Law Journal: 22, 3 (2013). 758.

Metzner, Ralph. *Germanic Mythology and the Fate of Europe*. ReVision: 13, 1 (Summer 1990). 17.

Van Caenegem, R.C. *The Modernity of Medieval Law*. Legal History Review: 68, 3 (September 2000). 318.

Van Caenegem, R.C. *The Modernity of Medieval Law*. Legal History Review: 68, 3 (September 2000). 320.

Chapter IV - Works Consulted

Beckwith, Christopher I. *The Actual Achievements of Early Indo-Europeans, in Accurate Historical Context*. Cliodynamics, The Journal of Theoretical & Mathematical History: 4, 1 (January 2013). 44-53.

Benham, Jenny. *Law or Treaty? Defining the Edge of Legal Studies in the Early and High Medieval Periods*. Historical Research: 86, 233 (August 2013). 487-497.

Bennett, Judith. *Medieval Europe: A Short History*. McGraw-Hill Higher Education: 11th Edition (2011).

Bisson, Thomas. *Cultures of Power, Lordship, Status, and Process in Twelfth-Century Europe*. University of Pennsylvania Press (1995).

Bullough, Donald A. *Recycling Charlemagne in the Fifteenth Century, North and South*. Early Medieval Europe: 12, 4 (Dec. 2003).

Carella, Bryan. *Evidence for Hiberno-Latin Thought in the Prologue to the Laws of Alfred*. Studies in Philology: 108, 1 (Winter 2011). 1-26.

DeGregorio, Scott. *Affective Spirituality: Theory and Practice in Bede and Alfred the Great*. Essays in Medieval Studies: 22, 1 (February 2006).

Faulkner, Thomas. *Carolingian Kings and the Leges Barbarorum*. Historical Research: 86, 233 (August 2013). 443-464.

Gozzi, Gustavo. *History of International Law and Western Civilization*. International Community Law Review: 9, 4 (December 2007), 353-373.

Innes, Matthew. The *Classical Tradition in the Carolingian Renaissance: Ninth-Century Encounters with Suetonius*. International Journal of the Classical Traditio: 3, 3 (Winter 1997). 265-283.

Jurasinski, Stefan. *Sanctuary, House-Peace, and the Traditionalism of Alfred's Laws*. Journal of Legal History: 31, 2 (August 2010). 129-147.

Leitch, Stephanie. *The Wild Man, Charlemagne and the German Body*. Art History: 31, 3 (June 2008). 283-302.

Madden, M. Stuart. *Paths of Western Law After Justinian*. Widener Law Journal: 22, 3 (2013). 757-828.

Metzner, Ralph. *Germanic Mythology and the Fate of Europe*. ReVision: 13, 1 (Summer 1990). 16-28.

Ostrogorsky, George. *History of the Byzantine State*. New Brunswick, NJ: Rutgers University Press (1969).

Rose, Jonathan. *The Rule of Law in the Western World: An Overview*. Journal of Social Philosophy: 35, 4 (Winter 2004). 457-470.

Stofferahn, Steven. *Staying the Royal Sword: Alcuin and the Conversion Dilemma in Early Medieval Europe*. Historian: 71, 3 (Fall 2009). 461-480.

Van Caenegem, R.C. *The Modernity of Medieval Law*. Legal History Review: 68, 3 (September 2000). 313-329.

Yorke, Barbara, Derek Gore, Sarah Hamilton, Nicholas Higham, Jim Bolton, R.A. Higham, Christopher Allmand, G.A. Loud, John France, Norman Housley, Simon Barton, and Nige Saul. *Medieval. History*: 89, 296 (October 2004). 625-637.

Chapter V

The Triumph of Law from the English Glorious Revolution and the Influence of the Reformation and Counter Reformation

Historiography

Introduction

English common law was developed over many years beginning with the importation of Roman law and locally developed by its earliest lawgivers, such as Edward the Confessor (1005-1066 CE), who in his early years received much of his legal knowledge during his exile in continental Europe. Edward conveyed such experiences to England when he became its ruler in 1042 CE and memorialized England's laws and customs. Significant developments followed in laws requiring increased royal power-sharing and the recognition of the barons' rights in the *Magna Carta* in 1215 CE, which attempted to limit the arbitrary rulings of the English monarchs.[54]

These themes continued throughout England's history, leading to the Glorious Revolution of 1688 CE. We will examine the stages of English *common law* from its beginnings through the Glorious Revolution, highlighting developments in parliamentary government. Further, we will argue that English law is bolstered by these events being counterintuitive to the relative turmoil brought on by the revolution, distinguishing it from previous academic research.

1. The End of the Renaissance

The Glorious Revolution marks the end of the Renaissance period in Britain, leading to the legal philosophies of the Enlightenment that are seminal to modern concepts of human rights, deliberative government and the pursuit of life, liberty and property. The Glorious Revolution is a watershed event in Britain's history, marking the end of its Renaissance period and transitioning into its Enlightenment period. It is also referred to by historians as the Revolution of 1688, or the Bloodless Revolution. It is called "bloodless" because some argue that it

---

[54] Encyclopaedia Britannica Online, *Glorious Revolution*, last modified May 9, 2016, https://www.britannica.com/event/Glorious-Revolution

resulted in a peaceful transfer of power without the need for major conflict and allowed the 'rule of law' to prevail.[55]

James II (1633-1701 CE), the last of the Stuart house and a Roman Catholic, was elevated to the King of Great Britain (including Scotland and Ireland) from 1685 CE to 1688 CE when he abdicated the throne. By the time James was installed as king, England had been entrenched in Anglicanism since Henry VIII (1491-1547 CE) broke from Roman Catholicism and established the Church of England, including his annulled marriage from the Catholic Queen Catherine of Aragon (1485-1536 CE) in 1533 CE.[56]

James II's Catholicism was a shock to most of England which remained mainly Anglican for over 150 years. James was not simply Roman Catholic, but worked zealously to reverse the progress of the Reformation when he assumed power. At the time, there existed penal laws against any religion other than the Church of England. One of James' first acts as king was to issue a Declaration of Indulgence in 1687 CE. According to John Jolliffe, "James issued an order in Council on May 4th, 1687, requiring the bishops to have the Declaration read out in all the churches and chapels in their dioceses."[57] He further observes that, "Its real purpose...was to facilitate the pre-eminence of the Roman Catholic Church."[58] This action did not sit well with the Anglican bishops and members of the British Parliament, who vigorously resisted James' demands.

Both clergy and politicians united against James and made a plea to Prince William of Orange (1650-1702 CE) to intervene. William was James' Protestant nephew, son-in-law and heir who resided in the Dutch Republic. William gained his reputation among Protestants by fighting against the Catholic powers in Europe, especially France. By November 6, 1688, William marched on London with up to 21,000 troops, including many Catholics. Consequently, by December 11th James fled

---

[55] Ibid. Britannica, *Glorious Revolution*
[56] Ibid. Britannica, *Glorious Revolution*
[57] James P. Pfiffner, *The Contemporary Presidency: Magna Carta and the Contemporary Presidency* (Presidential Studies Quarterly, 46, 1: March 2016), 47.
[58] Ibid. Pfiffner, 47.

Whitehall Palace, abandoning his throne. William eventually ascended as king, replacing James.[59]

This is just the beginning of the history of the Glorious Revolution. The historical significance of England's fight against its legitimate king lies in how its Parliament addressed the aftermath of James' abdication. The newly assembled Parliament drafted the Bill of Rights of 1689 that had far-reaching influence on political and philosophical thought, leading into the Age of Enlightenment.[60]

2. The Development of Law In England

Taking a step back to review the development of law and legal practices in England since its inception; it starts with three main foundations of law that supported the stability of Western civilization as it emerged from the turbulent years after the collapse of the Western Roman Empire. These three main foundations are: Roman law (as conveyed by the Byzantine Empire through Justinian's Code, *Corpus Juris Civilis*, which was lost after the 6th century and rediscovered in the 11th), Germanic law (which is a hybrid of Roman and Gothic tribal customs) and *canon law* of the Catholic Church, which carries its traditions from Biblical teachings and Roman law.[61]

Roman law waned during the Early Middle Ages, but remained influential even combining with Germanic law. The Germanic tribes, although in control of most of Western Europe, greatly respected Roman civilization and sought to emulate some of its major customs, including its legal practices under Roman law. Over the one-thousand year period from 500 to 1500 CE, Europe's legal system progressed from its Roman roots, assimilated Germanic traditions and incorporated Christian morality and ethics. Along with the social upheavals brought about by the Black Death and the empowerment of Europe's bourgeoisie class, power-sharing began to move from monarchs to wider popular consent, as seen in the establishment of the jury system and early forms of

---

[59] Encyclopaedia Britannica Online, *Glorious Revolution*, last modified May 9, 2016, https://www.britannica.com/event/Glorious-Revolution
[60] Ibid. Britannica, *Glorious Revolution*
[61] Encyclopaedia Britannica Online, *European Law*, last modified June 19, 2008, https://www.britannica.com/topic/European-law

parliament. Such progress would later coalesce into Western law in practice today. Western law, resulting from these foundations introduced concepts that are often the goals of many modern nations, which include: limited and balanced governmental powers, civil and individual liberty, free economic markets and self-determination that empower citizens over governments.[62]

Van Caenegem declares that the medieval legal system made two significant contributions to Western law: the jury and popular representation. He states, "Just as democratic as the jury, but this time rooted in medieval Roman law, is the notion that matters which concern the whole community ought to be decided by all its members."[63] In this, the foundations of early parliaments were laid. Kings who previously issues decrees or convened private councils had to contend with nobles demanding popular participation in government. This was coupled with the large scale death and depopulation caused by the Black Plague's colossal impact on Europe's political, social and economic systems. People rebelled against the social-economic system forever after, sparking a spirit of revolt against the crushing system of serfdom. Nobles had to contend with this popular sentiment from that point forward, leading to later improvements in the management of the nobility's estates and the acceptance of popular involvement in government in the form of parliament.

England, however, was not as principally influenced as the continental European states that used *civil law*, because it had already developed its own legal standards by the time the Justinian Code was revived. England produced its own laws, called common law. As stated earlier, however, it must be noted that English law was also shaped by Roman law thanks to its earliest lawgivers, such as Edward the Confessor (circa. 1005-1066)[64] as previously noted.

Feudalism in England was dramatically altered after the adoption of the *Magna Carta* in 1215 CE, when nobles sought additional rights from

---

[62] Encyclopaedia Britannica Online, *European Law*, last modified June 19, 2008, https://www.britannica.com/topic/European-law

[63] R.C. van Caenegem, *The Modernity of Medieval Law*, (Legal History Review, 68, 3: September 2000), 320.

[64] Encyclopaedia Britannica Online, *European Law*, last modified June 19, 2008, https://www.britannica.com/topic/European-law

the king, especially regarding limits to arbitrary government and power sharing. By 1645 CE, England's Parliament effectively abolished feudalism and adopted many of the practices borrowed from the legacies of Roman law. Parallel to developments in continental Europe, English feudalism began to wane due to the obvious shortfalls in legal clarity under English common law and European feudal law.[65]

With the advent of the Renaissance and the Age of Enlightenment, law principles again changed. By the end of the 17th century, the idea of natural rights permeated Enlightenment-age philosophy and found its way into the legal concepts of human rights, self-evident and unalienable rights of humanity that were not provided by any person, sovereign or legal system, but are universal and freely inherent in human existence. Later, popular revolutions in America and France would fuel even greater change to law practices. Philosophical leaders in this area were John Locke (1632-1704 CE) and Thomas Hobbes (1588-1679 CE), who wrote extensively on the natural rights of man, classical republicanism and liberal theory, which fueled the parliamentary process in England and later influenced the American Revolution.[66]

This leads us to the more specific discussion of English common law and its impact on the Glorious Revolution of 1688. According to Potter, "The common law of England has been compared to a broad river with many tributaries or to a tree with many deep roots and myriad branches...its authority depends on its antiquity, on its ability to change and on popular involvement and public acceptability."[67]

It appears that the native Celts had little or no influence on common law. Britain's population is a study in tribal conquests and transformation. First, the Anglo-Saxons replaced the Britons. The Vikings wreaked havoc along England's shores and applied *Dane law*, which did not hold for long. Lastly, the Normans under William the Conqueror unified England in the 11th century, but it was under Henry II (1133-1189 CE) that *common law* coalesced.[68]

---

[65] Ibid. Britannica, *European Law*
[66] Ibid. Britannica, *European Law*
[67] Harry Potter, *Liberty and the Common Law* (History Today, 65, 12: Dec. 2015), 19.
[68] Encyclopaedia Britannica Online, *European Law*, last modified June 19, 2008, https://www.britannica.com/topic/European-law

Prior to this, there existed separate, uncoordinated legal systems. Henry II led the reform of England's legal system which included the amassing of power for the throne. Despite this, throughout the 12th and 13th centuries, England's system of courts became more uniform; judges and lawyers were trained effectively in common law and the jury system was retained. It was these reforms that proved their worth and ultimately led to the curtailing of royal power through the *Magna Carta* in 1215 CE. The promotion and support of the jury system has many valuable features that make commoners key to the system of justice. It quelled violence between parties and reduced vigilantism. Juries replaced the posse, where vengeance was transformed into justice. This is a significant transfer of historical power from God, kings and bureaucrats to the people - the beginning of a revolutionary age for the common man. This was a departure from continental European states, which still employed older forms of justice not necessarily invested in the people. England's legal system of common law continued to develop through the Middle Ages and the Early Modern Period.[69]

3. The Glorious Revolution

With this background, we can begin to examine how England's legal system and government managed through a major crisis of historic proportions. In 1688 CE, actions taken by England's King James II forced Britain into a revolution that included invasions from outside forces on what ironically became a well administered, self-governing country. Regardless, the Glorious Revolution of 1688, as Robin Clifton points out, "…is termed 'Glorious' not least for the smooth and bloodless manner of its accomplishment."[70] This event tested England's "rule of law" and its legal system's "due process".

This is not to say that this period came without its intrigues and mayhem. In fact, preceding the Revolution many Brits were alarmed during James II's brother and predecessor, Charles II's (1630-1685 CE) reign, as he also was a supporter of Catholicism and France. In 1672

---

[69] Encyclopaedia Britannica Online, *European Law*, last modified June 19, 2008, https://www.britannica.com/topic/European-law
[70] Robin Clifton, *James II's Two Rebellions* (History Today, 38, 7: July 1988), 23.

CE, Charles also issued a Royal Declaration of Indulgence which suspended all punitive laws against Catholics and dissenters of the Church of England. This did not sit well with traditional Anglican loyalists, including the English philosopher John Locke (1632-1704 CE). Locke is implicated in the Rye House Plot fomented to assassinate Charles II and James II in 1683 CE, ridding England of its pro-Catholic monarchs. Charles II was installed as king after the English Civil War and the resulting confusion at the death of Oliver Cromwell (1599-1658 CE). England sought to restore the monarchy and Charles II's father was the last king to rule England before the civil war. Charles added to his plotters' anger by dissolving the Parliament in 1681 CE. Locke wrote two treatises of government, one against patriarchal absolutism and the second an egalitarian argument that governments that ignore the people can be overthrown, which was essentially a call for revolution against Charles II. In these treatises, we see the future influence that Locke has on revolutionaries in the American Colonies across the Atlantic. Lest we believe Locke to be a complete radical, David Wootton observes that, "Locke's positions changed over time, and that Locke was indeed briefly a radical, between 1681 and 1688."[71] This illustrates the tension caused by the policies of Charles II, and by virtue of his relationship to Charles, the affect it had on James.

Religion, however, wasn't the only cause for concern among the British. Later in the 1750s, David Hume (1711-1776 CE), a Scottish philosopher, in his *History of Great Britain*, lauded the Glorious Revolution of 1688 not only on religious grounds, but what he felt more importantly was the introduction of a limited monarchy and more popular involvement through Parliament. Herein lays the essential argument of why the Glorious Revolution was so pivotal in English and, we daresay, global history: It was a contest between two notions of government, one from the past in monarchy and one for the future in the parliamentary process.

A series of errors made by Charles, and ultimately James, led the English to rebel against their King and permanently invoked the parliamentary process going forward. After Charles' dubious reign, it

---

[71] David Wootton, *John Locke and Richard Ashcraft's Revolutionary Politics* (Political Studies, 40, 1: March 1992), 97.

appeared to the English people that James wielded his authority unlawfully. Beginning in 1685 CE, James suppressed a rebellion in the West Country where show trials sent over 1,000 people to either their execution or deportation as slave laborers. The Monmouth Rebellion was a failed attempt by its Protestant Duke, who was an illegitimate son of James' brother and predecessor Charles, who challenged James. After this, James worked to improve the lot of Catholics by defying English law, making appointments of Catholics to military and naval commands and allowing them to become fellows at Protestant universities. This was all illegal under British law. Regardless, James suppressed resistance ruthlessly, leading to his further curtailing of power in Parliament when the House of Commons did not support his pro-Catholic policies. James revoked Parliament's Test Acts and Penal Laws affecting Catholics. The Test Acts required military and naval officers to be obedient to the Anglican Church. The Penal Laws punished anyone not attending Anglican Church observances or attending non-Anglican churches. These actions led to James' demand in 1687 that the Anglican bishops read his Declaration of Indulgence, which was perceived by the masses as his illegal support of Catholicism.

In 1688 CE, seven bishops defied his demand stating that it was illegal. James retaliated by holding another series of show trials, but even with a hand-picked jury, the bishops were acquitted. This was a serious test of English loyalty to their monarchy. Resulting from this, those in Parliament disaffected by James invited the Dutch William of Orange (1650-1702 CE) to invade England and restore the Protestant monarchy. Under the popular dissention to James' policies, James' army crumbled prior to the invasion, providing no opposition to William and thus ending James' reign as he fled England. According to Pincus, "...the English people, led by... Parliament, changed the English polity in only the most modest of ways in 1688-89. They slightly altered the succession, making it illegal for a Catholic ever to inherit the throne and passing the Toleration Act allowing Protestant Nonconformists to worship freely."[72] So, while James' efforts to liberate Catholics failed, religious toleration for non-Anglicans was achieved. In fact, William of Orange was not even Anglican, but Dutch Reformed. He was made

---

[72] Steven Pincus, *A Fight for the Future*, (History Today, 59, 10: October 2009), 11.

King of England in 1689 CE. Catholics, however, were further barred from public office.

The most important outcomes of this essentially peaceful revolt is not only the ascension of Parliament and the ruling body of Britain's government, or that of disallowing a non-Protestant from wearing the English Crown, but the production of the English Bill of Right in 1689 CE. The Bill of Rights is an Act of Parliament that declared specific limits to the powers of the monarchy and empowered the Parliament with additional rights not to be infringed by the Crown; that it should meet regularly, hold free elections and be protected while in Parliament. It protected freedom of speech and outlawed cruel and unusual punishment. All of these crucial rights were overstepped by James and Charles at one point or another, promoting Parliament's reaction.

The Bill of Rights of 1689 is the culmination of many years of England's social changes and the consistent drive of its leaders, both religious and secular, to maintain moral and legal justification for its actions. Nobles and preachers pointed to British history to explain the events of the Glorious Revolution. According to Key, "Preachers...used occasional or state sermons to explain contemporary upheavals from the perspective of God's law, Natural law, and Civil law."[73] Britain endured the tumultuous reign of James II and established the Bill of Rights in 1689 CE to restrict the monarchy from indiscriminate power and invest more sovereignty with the Parliament and the people. The Bill of Rights is the bedrock of the British Constitution and five out of thirteen Articles are still in use today. James succeeded in disaffecting the governing establishment of England. His attempts to reconstitute Catholicism alienated nobles and clergy alike.

4. The English Bill of Rights

As discussed earlier, this reached a climax when the ruling classes called for William of Orange to forcibly assume power and remove James from the throne. Upon doing so, William ordered an election of

---

[73] Newton Key, *The "Boast of Antiquity": Pulpit Politics Across the Atlantic Archipelago during the Revolution of 1688*, (Church History, 83, 3: September 2014), 618.

leaders to a national convention to decide England's governmental future. They declared James absent by abdication, which justified the convention. They were careful not to call it a Parliament because there was no legitimate reigning monarch. The Lords and Commons agreed to a procedural process and discussions began. The convention chose William and his cousin Mary II (1622-1694 CE), also a Protestant, to replace James and rule jointly as co-regents of the British Empire, which includes England, Scotland and Ireland.[74] The convention drafted a Declaration of Rights and presented it to William and Mary in February 1689 CE.

The Declaration that became the Bill of Rights of 1689 contained the following three major components:

1. Enumerating the offenses of James II
2. Confirming the rights of Parliament and presenting cures to James' offenses
3. Presenting the royal authority to William and Mary as the rightful rulers of Britain and establishing that Catholics, or those married to Catholics, are forbidden from ruling Britain

The Declaration of Rights was not meant to be promulgated as a law itself, but used as a basis for future legislation by Parliament. Nonetheless, the Declaration was ratified as a Bill ten months after its inception in December of 1689 CE. While curtailing arbitrary power of the crown was fundamental to the Bill of Rights, Geoffrey Lock underscores its most important significance by stating, "Above all, it incorporated and reaffirmed the principle that parliamentary consent was needed for legislation and taxation."[75] Goldie goes further to observe, "The Bill decreed that parliaments should be convened frequently and that their proceedings should be immune from interference, that elections should be free, and that taxation should be subject to parliamentary control."[76] It is widely recognized by historians and political scientists

---

[74] Encyclopaedia Britannica Online, *Glorious Revolution*, last modified May 9, 2016, https://www.britannica.com/event/Glorious-Revolution

[75] Geoffrey Lock, *The 1689 Bill of Rights* (Political Studies, 37, 4: December 1989), 561.

[76] Mark Goldie, *The Bill of Rights, 1689 and 1998* (History Today, 48, 9: September 1998), 10.

that the Bill of Rights of 1689 are advancement in the parliamentary process, whereby specific consent is agreed upon between the governors and the governed. Later in 1791 CE, the United States' colonies drafted a similar Bill of Rights as amendments to the United States Constitution that, in some cases, are identically worded.

5. Aftermath of the Glorious Revolution

Not all historians agree, however, that the Glorious Revolution is completely without shortcomings. The Revolution turned back James' efforts to allow religions other than Anglicanism, but mainly Catholicism, to participate in government and military affairs. In cementing Protestantism within the Bill of Rights of 1689, the Parliament reduced freedom of conscience that James' policies advanced. The Toleration Act of 1689 further marginalized Catholics in that it allowed what were called Dissenters (from Anglican theology) such as Baptists, Congregationalists, Anabaptists, Puritans and many others to have religious freedom form Anglican dominance, but kept Catholics barred from government and military participation. That said, it was primarily devised to make clear that state interference in religion was outlawed. The additional upside of this Act was the ongoing progress of the principle of separation of church and state, fundamental to American independence a century later.[77]

The legend of the Glorious Revolution in historiography relies mainly on Edmund Burke's *Reflections* from 1790, who compared the undertakings of 1688-89 with previous revolutions (like the English Civil War of the mid-1600s) and revolutions in contemporary France that are more violent and bloody. It is in this interpretation that the Glorious Revolution gets its name, including the term 'Bloodless' Revolution, as Burke viewed it as a peaceful process that reestablished the principles of the *Magna Carta* and subsequent English constitutions.

In recent years, this version of history has been challenged by modern historians. Some view William's use of the military as a Dutch invasion of England not for the purpose of reconstituting English law, but of

---

[77] W. Brown Patterson, *The Glorious Revolution Reconceived* (Sewanee Review, 119, 2: Spring, 2011), 330-333.

allying with France. William's naval fleet and forces of up to 21,000 troops was one of the largest amassed in English history. Had James decided to stay and fight, it could have amounted to one of the bloodiest conflicts in England. It is also pointed out that during this period carnage did occur in Scotland in the Battles of Killiecrankie and Boyne, the Massacre of Glencoe and in Ireland at the Battle of Aughrim, casting doubt that the Glorious Revolution was completely bloodless. Despite this perspective, Ted Vallence critiques that, "Burke may have been wrong to represent the revolution of 1688 as a peaceful and smooth process but ultimately he may have been right that it was this revolution which created the conditions that ensured England did not go down the same road as France in the late eighteenth century."[78] Given this, England avoided the significant turmoil and bloodshed that affected France during the French Revolution (1789-1799 CE), while it established equitable governance for commoners and nobility alike.

6. Conclusion

In assessing the events of 1688-89 CE, it becomes unmistakably clear that the Glorious Revolution, was not a single historical event, but a culmination of the efforts of the British who were steadfastly committed to the 'rule of law'. To test this hypothesis, an assessment of Britain's landmark legal proceedings is important. Over an 800-year period, English law developed in response to certain social dynamics. In 1215 CE, the 'divine right of kings' was challenged in a peace accord between the crown and barons who sought greater say in how they were governed. John I (1166-1216 CE) was a king who callously ruled England, leading to the nobles' rebellion. John believed in his absolute privilege to reign as he saw fit and embroiled England in endless wars, taxed the barons mercilessly and challenged the church. His actions provoked a popular uprising that was expressed in 63 demands contained in a document called the *Magna Carta*, meaning in Latin "the Great Charter". As a result, John turned his own army unsuccessfully on the barons. The barons united and prepared for armed conflict with the king,

---

[78] Ted Vallance, *The Unrevolutionary Revolution? Interpreting the Revolution of 1688* (Teaching History, 151: June 2013), 19.

making specific demands that were enumerated in the document. The *Magna Carta* honorably requested that King John provide for greater freedoms and latitude with the barons, sharing social and economic opportunity during the harsh feudal period. Despite his initial resistance, John acquiesced to a monumental underpinning of the 'rule of law' contained within the charter. As Eskridge III discerns: "Unwittingly...King John gave sanction to that most venerable of institutions—the rule of law—while forever placing himself and his successors within its bounds."[79] From this point forward, the monarchs of England would honor and obey the laws of the land. Behavior deemed illegal by the people was considered intolerable and subject to the law for correction. In the face of absolutism found so prevalent in the monarchy, this was a massive advancement in governing arbitrary power and requiring *due process* under the law. These are terms and conditions we mindlessly expect and rely on today.

Another clause addressed the concept of *habeas corpus* which outlawed unlawful search, seizure and imprisonment, making law superior to arbitrariness so fundamental to free societies. It also included freedom of religion, because the Catholic Church was harassed by John and the barons saw to it that it remained free of imperial interference. After John's passing, the *Magna Carta* was reaffirmed by successor king and by the late 1600s, when governance once again required correction; it led to the Glorious Revolution.

England's *Magna Carta* laid the foundation for legal defining moments in both British and American history. Prior to the Glorious Revolution is the *Mayflower Compact* of 1620 CE that instituted a provisional government for the Puritans who landed in the New World. From there the American Colonies grew in size and required more complex laws to manage their affairs. Eskridge notes, *"The Body of Liberties of the Massachusets Collonie in New England was the first attempt at a written legal code."*[80] As England dealt with its legal concerns, the American Colonies were also facing their own governmental challenges and looked to the 'rule of law' to answer

---

[79] Charles R. Eskridge III, *Modern Lessons from Original Steps Towards the American Bill of Rights* (Texas Review of Law & Politics, 19, 1: Fall, 2014), 29.
[80] Ibid. Eskridge, pg. 34.

serious concerns regarding the British Monarchy's stance on colonial matters. Like England, the American Colonies perceived the crown dispensing arbitrary taxation, military interference and mock trials as abhorrent. By 1770 CE, less than one century after the Glorious Revolution, the American Colonies were faced with very similar circumstances. Try as they might, the colonials did not change King George III's (1738-1820 CE) position and their opposition was met with force at the Boston Massacre, where American civilians were killed by British soldiers. This event launched the American War of Independence which was justified by the colonial leaders' efforts to provide a sound legal footing for the rebellion against King George. From this is derived the Declaration of Independence of 1774 CE, the United States Constitution and the Bill of Rights in 1789 CE, exactly 100 years after the Glorious Revolution.

What these events bear out is that despite monumental historical trials from monarchs, militaries and social upheavals, British common law has endured because of the application of the 'rule of law' and 'due process' of the law found in major historical junctures like the Glorious Revolution and others. From there, Western Civilization has spread its concepts of limited government, human freedom and equality. Certainly, it is an ideal that human beings are at their best when they are free, which has prevailed at certain times and societies throughout the ages. It is the concepts of natural law, human rights, equality, fair representation and ultimately the freedom of humanity that are vital steps in the progress of Western society and humanity. It is these notions that inspired the *Magna Carta*, Humanism in the Middle Ages, the English Glorious Revolution of 1688 and The Declaration of Independence. Human freedom has faced down tyranny and opened the human spirit to unprecedented creativity and the triumph of law.

Background

The Renaissance and Reformation cover a long period extending from the 14th century CE to the 18th century CE. Since the Medieval Period has been previously discussed, the focus of this section will be for the period beginning in the early 16th century to the 18th century CE.

The Renaissance and Reformation is an extensive topic and there are multiple historical avenues that can be studied as is the case with most of history. To retain some focus, the early Renaissance was partially responsible for the events of the Reformation. The dawn of Humanism inspired philosophers, academics and theologians to ponder alternatives to the strict doctrines and obvious flaws within the church. While there are many factors that caused European culture to attempt to reorder society after the chaos of the preceding centuries, the large scale death and depopulation caused by the Black Plague's cataclysmic impact on Europe's political, social and economic systems was indeed another major factor. People rebelled against the old social-economic systems thereafter.

Given Italy's geographic location and seafaring role, it was heavily impacted by the Black Plague. Its major population centers were devastated and in the aftermath people began to question the exclusively religious focus on the afterlife and contemplated living in the here and now. The church appeared powerless in the face of the pestilence and brought much doubt into the minds of Italy's new leaders and thinkers, especially in Florence.

From Florence emerged the Medici banking family, led by Lorenzo de' Medici (1449-1492 CE), a great patron of the arts of whom Michelangelo (1475-1564 CE) and Leonardo (1452-1519 CE) were artisans; who captured the spirit of Europe's rebirth in their art, sculpture and architecture. Florence also contributed literary scholars such as Niccolo Machiavelli (1469-1527 CE), who's work *The Prince* is considered foundational to modern political science. From here arose new concepts in humanism (focus on man) as opposed to the God-centric philosophies of the Middle Ages. As such, we can readily see these changes more as a movement having seismic and widespread effects rather than simply identifying historical changes as in other periods.

From Florence, the Renaissance was exported throughout Europe via many avenues and venues. Burke comments on two such vehicles: portraits and autobiographies. He states, "The analogy between portraits and biographies – or between self-portraits and autobiographies – will be obvious and has indeed often been pointed out. So has the fact that these genres developed in Renaissance Italy, followed, usually at a certain distance, in other parts of Europe." [81]

Mapmaking was also a burgeoning skill that produced maps as a popular consumer good. Carlton makes it abundantly clear in her dissertation that maps sold as a popular consumer good began in Renaissance Italy. Maps were no longer the sole property of cartographers and navigators. Populations began to observe the material world around them and study the natural sciences. She observes, "Just as family portraits were commissioned to emphasize desirable characteristics, maps became a short-hand way to show one's connection to a place or knowledge about the world. In this way, maps became a new form of cultural capital in the sixteenth century...."[82]

Within this context we can see emerging from Renaissance Italy several attempts to evolve from what was perceived as the religious, political and cultural chaos of the Middle Ages. While the Middle Ages (erroneously termed the Dark Ages) continued many cultural developments, devastating social conditions such as the Black Plague had significant influence on Europe; and most importantly Italy, where many of the Renaissance's creative beginnings arose and exploded into sweeping changes throughout Europe.

Political, religious and social systems were widely impacted by the Black Death and its subsequent psychological consequences on the European populace. There was large scale death and depopulation caused by the Black Plague. People rebelled against the previous social order, most importantly against the crushing system of serfdom. Nobles had to contend with this popular sentiment from that point forward

---

[81] Peter Burke, *Jack Goody and the Comparative History of Renaissances* (Theory Culture and Society, 26, 16: 2009), 20.
[82] Genevieve Carlton, *Worldly Consumers: The Demand for Maps in Renaissance Italy* (Ph.D. diss. Northwestern University: 2011), 3.

leading to later improvements in the management of the nobility's estates and the acceptance of popular involvement in government. Along with the social upheavals brought about by the Black Death was the empowerment of Europe's bourgeoisie class. Power sharing began to move from monarchs to wider popular consent, as also seen in the establishment of the jury system and early forms of parliament.

MacCulloch also points out that the theology of Purgatory was bolstered by the Black Death because, "It gave people a sense that they had some control over death...."[83] This also served to provide order in a vastly chaotic period. The lay people (as opposed to the clergy who were devastated in numbers after the Plague) took greater control of the prayer component of Christian worship and the self-mortification movement rose significantly, along with the cult of the saints, pilgrimages and the growth of charitable and welfare activities. There was a newly inspired interest in Christ's humanity as he suffered much like the European population at this time. These changes set the grounds for even greater changes to come throughout the Renaissance and Reformation.

After the Middle Ages and the Black Death, many factors contributed to the restoration of Europe, which included: the reform of Christianity that manifested through the Reformation, and the redistribution of power to the bourgeois class that led to the beginnings of parliamentary rule and the expansion of thought and expression as presented by the Renaissance Humanists. It can be observed that of all the contributors to Europe's rebirth in the Early Modern Period, it was the explosion of thought and expression that was the most significant catalyst of change.

Humanism was a movement embedded in the very fabric of learned culture and society. Beginning in Italy, it was a new appreciation of the scholarship and wisdom found in ancient classical times and a reaction to the narrowness that was applied by restrictive church doctrines. We know that universities grew across Europe. According to Burke, "...Italian universities of the 15th and 16th centuries, [were taught by] *humanista*...The point of the name was the claim that the study of these

---

[83] Diarmaid MacCulloch, *The Reformation, A History* (New York: Penguin, 2003), 13.

subjects (notably rhetoric, ethics and history) made the students more human."[84]

Beginning with Petrarch's rediscovery of Cicero (106 - 43 BCE), who was a thinker and politician from ancient Rome, early humanists revived the advances of ancient civilization. Thought leaders and patrons of the arts vaunted such works and were hungry for more. Later, thinkers like the Florentine Niccolo Machiavelli furthered the spread of classical values through his many famous literary works. After the fall of Constantinople in 1453 CE, many Byzantine scholars also carried into Europe much of what was preserved there from antiquity. There was a confluence of cultural influences throughout this period that worked to infuse Europe with new ideas and break from the long past, from the fall of Rome through the Middle Ages. The list of prominent humanists is extensive.

The efforts of humanists may not have had sudden and immediate sway on major institutions like the church or traditional scholarship, but the pervasive and long-term growth of humanist thinking laid the foundation for a burgeoning civilization built on new forms of art, architecture, science, literature and political thought. According to MacCulloch, "Humanists were lovers and connoisseurs of words. They saw them as containing the power which could be used actively to change human society for the better."[85] In hindsight, we can confidently say that their efforts did advance European culture.

Future European society was also affected by the pen and the sword; however, the sword determined the key geographic and religious tolerance boundaries that designate Europe's geopolitical landscape to this day, which makes the sword most prominent, but its humanist roots romanticize the changes created during the Renaissance.

The new freedom of thought brought about by Renaissance thinkers, clerics, universities and monarchs indeed opened completely new avenues for societal behavior. Furthering change, it was Martin Luther's call for reform and the church's practice of collecting taxes from local princes that not only brought into question the behaviors of the church

---

[84] Peter Burke, *Jack Goody and the Comparative History of Renaissances* (Theory Culture and Society, 26, 16: 2009), 22.
[85] Diarmaid MacCulloch, *The Reformation, A History* (New York, Penguin: 2003), 77.

regarding earthly wealth and the practice of indulgences, but also deeply challenged long held theological principles like *sola fide* (Latin: by faith alone). The church's practice of selling indulgences appeared to delegate to men the ability to mitigate God's justice in the afterlife and its collection of taxes pressured European economies.

MacCulloch points out that during the Middle Ages the Mass and Purgatory were pillars of the church.[86] Luther noted that the Bible's New Testament only referenced heaven and hell. Church thinkers had developed the concept of Purgatory as a middle space between heaven and hell against what Luther believed to be strict biblical context. Moreover, the church literally capitalized on this condition by selling indulgences that would mitigate time spent in Purgatory speeding the faithful to heaven. MacCulloch goes on to say [referencing the doctrine of Purgatory] that, "It was possible to do something about one's salvation – this was precisely the doctrine which Martin Luther was to make a particular target after 1517."[87]

Luther and many other church reformers called for the abolition of this doctrine and stated that by faith alone are we saved by God. So, we see from this stark contrast of theological thought that battle lines were drawn in Europe as the Reformation also took on geopolitical ramifications. German princes seized upon this to break from the church's taxation, which was crushing their ability to economically survive. Out of this, a bourgeois class of peasants saw this as further opportunity to rise out of the limits of the feudal system, seeking greater autonomy. Europe's north and most importantly Germany (the Holy Roman Empire) quickly adopted Reformation principles and refrained from paying Rome church taxes.

Often overlooked in history is the *German Peasants' War*, where mass violence erupted across Germany. According to MacCulloch the German Peasants' War was, "…Europe's most massive and widespread popular uprising before the 1789 French Revolution."[88] While the revolts failed under the crushing check of the aristocracy, social change

---

[86] Diarmaid MacCulloch, *The Reformation, A History* (New York: Penguin, 2003), 10.
[87] Ibid. MacCulloch, pg. 15.
[88] Ibid. MacCulloch, pg. 158.

had already taken hold. The spark of reform that Luther ignited further enabled the populace to question the old hierarchical system.

What followed were a series of widespread and devastating wars from the early 1500s through the late 1600s that included the Eighty Years' War (1568-1648 CE), the French Wars of Religion (1562-1598 CE), the Thirty Years' War (1618-1648 CE), the Wars of the Three Kingdoms (1639-1651 CE) and several others that redefined Europe's geopolitical boundaries. MacCulloch refers to "confessional divisions"[89] of Europe along religious/geographic lines. Generally, Roman Catholic territories were located in the southwest and Lutheran/Reformed territories were located in the northeast, with pockets of other sects in between. It wasn't until the Peace of Westphalia (1648 CE) that the religious wars of Europe ended. Europe's sovereign territories took shape, ending the dream of the Holy Roman Empire where Europe would serve one rule for all of Christendom. MacCulloch sums it up well, "After 1648, there was no prospect that this foundation institution of the medieval Western Christendom was ever going to become a coherent, bureaucratic and centralized state...."[90] Europe's map today looks nearly as it did those many centuries ago.

After the social upheavals of the Late Middle Ages, the intelligentsia of Early Modern Europe sought different answers for earthly life outside the theological mainstream that was held by church authority and the scholasticism found in universities. MacCulloch shares that humanists of the Early Modern period realized, "...that there was more to life than the Middle Ages."[91] One of the catalysts was the refocus on antiquity as an age of enlightenment, learning and creativity not found at that time. Poets like Petrarch propounded the ancient works of Cicero, fueling a thirst for past knowledge. With the fall of Constantinople more ancient manuscripts became available for study in Western Europe.

Neoplatonism was the study of Plato's philosophy given his rediscovery. Throughout the Middle Ages, the availability of Aristotle's thought was more available, therefore, more readily studied in Western European universities. The availability of Platonic thought, as

---

[89] Diarmaid MacCulloch, *The Reformation, A History* (New York: Penguin, 2003), 486.
[90] Ibid. MacCulloch, pg. 500.
[91] Ibid.MacCulloch, pg. 78.

Aristotle's teacher, was novel and made challenge of Aristotelian thought - and therefore, church philosophy - possible by humanists. Humanist thought took hold in the European universities, and during the Early Modern period growth of universities accelerated, contributing to the expansion of humanist concepts.

Additionally, the rediscovery of ancient manuscripts including fragments of hermitic literature and the Cabbala presented conceptual and spiritual alternatives to Christian orthodoxy. Humanists like Erasmus pushed for general reading of the Bible, which lent to critique of Biblical interpretation not in keeping with church authority. The invention of the printing press with moveable type fueled the distribution of Bibles, making them more accessible to the populace. As a result, scholars transitioned from copying manuscripts to dedicating more time to philosophical studies.

All of these things significantly moved European society, to broader studies of philosophical thought and Biblical interpretation, a challenge of Catholic Church teachings and ultimately the Reformation.

During the Early Modern Period, several dynamics were in play that created an environment to challenge then current Catholic Church hierarchy and teachings. We learn from MacCulloch that given the disruptions from the Avignon Papacy, which severely damaged the authority of the papal office and the movement for church reform that swept through Europe, church leaders and reformers sought to promote a, "collective authority rather than the single primacy of the Bishop of Rome"[92] called *conciliarism*. This concept was fiercely fought by the popes, and never gained enough support to take hold; and with the fall of Constantinople to the Ottomans, challenging Western church authority became unpopular. That said, the papacy remained under fierce scrutiny by reformers due to widespread simony and obvious corruption, but none of this lent more to its ultimate challenge than the doctrine of indulgences.

Henry VIII's (King of England, 1491-1509 CE) reign embodies the confluence of the church and state, the conflict between the Christian doctrines of the Catholic Church and that of the Reformers, the humanist movement and the inventions (moveable type printing press & paper)

---

[92] Ibid. MacCulloch, pg. 38.

that catalyzed broader reading of humanist works and the Bible by the laity. Early in Henry's rule, he was conferred the tile of "Defender of the Faith" by the Catholic Church and Pope Leo X for his literary contributions that supported the indissolubility of marriage and papal supremacy, which was a critical point as the Reformation was building momentum. Needless to say, the irony of this is one of history's greatest turnabouts. Not only did Henry defy the Catholic Church on the matter or marriage, but he took one of Europe's most dramatic actions against the Catholic Church by breaking England completely from Rome.

MacCulloch points out that, "The Roman bureaucracy, already infuriated with the English for their reluctance to help the effort to defend Europe against the Turks after the disaster of Mohacs, obstructed the annulment of the Aragon marriage....."[93] The Battle of Mohacs in 1526 CE between the Turks and the Kingdom of Hungary was a watershed event in that Europe lost a definitive battle to the Turks and had to partition Hungary, allowing further Turkish advancement into Europe. Due to Henry's inability to produce an heir through Catharine of Aragon, he became desperate to annul his marriage. With the Catholic Church preventing the annulment, Henry sought an alternative in the ancient theory that the King is the Supreme Head of the Church in their kingdom. This led Henry to ultimately break England's church from Rome in 1534 CE.

Beneath this monumental event played out many of the issues central to the Renaissance and Reformation. Thomas Cromwell, Henry's Chancellor, was one of England's most energetic Reform activists. Thomas Cranmer, the Archbishop of Canterbury, once a loyal Catholic churchman, according to MacCulloch began, "...hating the papacy and taking an interest in the Reformation's message."[94] Anne Boleyn, Henry's mistress and Queen after his annulment with Catherine, was a significant disciple of the Reform movement in England. With her new influence with Henry, she was able to import an increasing amount of Reformation literature into England. It was the dissemination of Reformation literature that had major influence on promoting reform in

---

[93] Ibid. MacCulloch, pg. 198.
[94] Ibid. MacCulloch, pg. 199.

England. This single act by Henry did much to connect the Renaissance and Reformation movements.

Maritime exploration and trade had the farthest religious reach and impact on subsequent generations. From the 1400s to the 1700s, European powers not only increased global trade through passages to India and other exotic ports, but established trade routes and discovered new lands as a result. With the sailors went religious missionaries, eager to spread the Word of God. Many of the expeditions were funded with this very expectation in mind, but little did the European monarchs and brave explorers know how monumental their efforts would be. According to Boorstin, "Within a few decades the European world concept would be transformed. The dominant Island of the Earth...was displaced by a dominant Ocean of the Earth...comprising two-thirds of the surface. Never before had the arena of human experience been so suddenly or so drastically revised."[95]

Navigators became famous for their extensive sailing accomplishments. For Portugal, Bartolomeu Dias and Vasco da Gama discovered the African coast and routes to India, Japan and Brazil. These discoveries became critical trading opportunities for European powers. For Spain, Christopher Columbus discovered the Americas, opening trading routes and opportunities for missionary activity, which is known as the Columbian Exchange, where vast quantities of food, people, livestock, religion and culture were exchanged between Europe and the Americas. The slave trade was also opened.

It was this age of exploration that ushered in European imperialism and colonialism. Native cultures were dominated culturally, economically and religiously. European powers including England, Spain, Portugal and France, through their navigation of the oceans advanced global domination of vast areas of Africa, North America and South America, brining European settlers, religion and culture which have had monumental bearing to this day.

The Catholic Church's reaction to Luther's protests was to repudiate his arguments. However, the strong sentiment against erred Catholic theology regarding indulgences, the cult of the Saints, its Biblical challenges regarding Faith Alone, and the challenge to church hierarchy

---

[95] Daniel J. Boorstin, *The Discoverers* (New York: Random House, 1985), 256.

on papal primacy, simony of the Cardinals and tax corruption, would not abate.

Universities were a hotbed for Reformation thinking and both clerical theologians like Luther and secular scholars like Erasmus were spreading its effects to the general populations of Europe. Only in the staunch Catholic countries of Portugal, Spain, Italy and France did Catholicism remain unchallenged, which required a degree of suppression. Protestantism and Protestants didn't enjoy a label of separated brethren as they were being deported resulting from the Catholic Inquisition. MacCulloch notes that, "As a result, [of Martin Luther's writings among *alumbrados*] the whole movement suffered a formal condemnation in September 1525."[96]

After its initial period of denial and Thomas Cajetan (1469 – 1534 CE) a leading Catholic cleric who led the efforts to suppress Luther by invoking the papal bull *Unigenitus* by Clement VI in 1343 CE to justify indulgences; Luther used Augustinian theology and philosophy and church law to defy Cajetan's reasoning and reject the Catholic Church's position. It was only after half of Europe's leaving the Catholic Church, seeking identity in the Reformation, that the Catholic Church realized it had to do more than suppress and reject Reformation initiatives. Consequently, Pope Paul III opened an ecumenical Council of Trent in 1545 CE in Trento, Italy, to respond to the Reformation and bring renewal to the Catholic Church. The Council of Trent featured the Catholic Church's complete response to the Reformation in what is historically called the Counter-Reformation. It addressed issues in Church theology, hierarchy, politics and evangelization. The Catholic Church wanted to win back Europe only after it faced certain separation and took a hard line against the Reformation. Hardly the response to one's separated brethren.

Enough cannot be said of Martin Luther's impact on Western civilization let alone whether he had more influence within or without the Catholic Church that he was resisting. To recount the various influences, we can observe the following:

---

[96] Diarmaid MacCulloch, *The Reformation, A History* (New York: Penguin, 2003), 65.

- His "95 Theses" caused the Catholic Church to first challenge and then condemn his thoughts. In either case, the force of his arguments prevailed. Both sides had to reform their positions.
- The practice of indulgences was uncovered to be non-Biblical and corrupt.
- Salvation was adjusted to be attainable directly from Christ without the need for a cult of Saints or human intermediaries.
- The reading of Scripture, through the proselytizing of Humanists and other preachers, caused laypeople to read the Bible directly without the need for clerical interpretation only.
- At the time, resistance to temporal papal power was perceived as positive because the papacy looked and acted like a corrupt state. By this challenge, the Popes had to draw more from their spiritual influence and less from their temporal power.
- Religious freedom increased and new sects proliferated, seeking their own philosophies to adhere to the Scripture.
- The Catholic Church had to undergo significant reforms itself to remain relevant to the modern world, changing hierarchical structure and its own traditional interpretations of Biblical teachings. To the extent that the Catholic Church reduced or eliminated untenable practices is a substantial improvement.
- The expansion and use of the printing press in the spreading of Luther's reform message. This had unprecedented and unlimited impact on the Early Modern Period and forward.

This is just to identify only a few of the relative impacts of Luther's reform challenge. It is evident that his influence effectively changed not only Reformation quarters, but the Catholic Church and, more broadly, Western Civilization.

From all this, it is very clear that the Catholic Church, after nearly imploding, decided it needed a concerted effort to respond to the Reformation. The reformers targeted very specific ecclesiastical, doctrinal and spiritual problems in the Catholic Church. As we've dealt with earlier, the Reformation was more about questioning key church doctrines and the absoluteness of the papacy. Abuses by the church became flagrant during the Early Modern Period, whether it was indulgences, simony, wealthy bishops, or church tax. All of these amounted to an easy critique for reformers who, after surviving the Black Death with little help from the church, could point to these abuses as cause for the need for drastic change.

On a doctrinal footing, reformers saw the church deviating from key Scriptural teachings. Sometimes referred to as the *five solas* (Latin for 'alone'), it was: Scripture alone (no extra-Biblical interpretations), faith alone (belief that only Jesus Christ saves), God's grace alone (works cannot save), Christ alone (no need for priestly intermediaries) and glory to God alone (the resistance to saints cult worship).

Regarding the Pope, reformers saw deep corruption in the Roman Curia; indulgences, simony, allegiance to secular powers, and the like. The papacy looked weak, worldly and decadent. This and the rise of nationalism throughout Europe, combined with a push toward conciliarism, gave cause to reject the Pope's primacy.

The Counter-Reformation had to deal with these issues and did so vigorously via the Council of Trent. It upheld that works *and* faith were keys to salvation, while supporting the venerable traditions like pilgrimages, the cult of the saints and the Real Presence in the Eucharist. It can be compared to rebranding in today's corporate marketing. With that said, improvements were made to unify the church hierarchy and uniformly educate priests to better serve the laity. MacCulloch states, "...the task of Catholic churchmen was to remold the multifarious patterns of medieval devotion and religious practice that might be considered vaguely Christian into a form compatible with the strategies laid down by the Council of Trent."[97] The pluralism of church orders was integrated and encouraged to provide counter arguments on behalf of the Catholic Church, which was widely done. Bishops were appointed for spiritual needs rather than political ones. There was significant spiritual renewal and an integrating of church doctrine and ecclesiastical organization. Major reforms re-entrenched the papacy, which was perceived as strongly leading the Catholic Church out of its blemished past. In all, the Counter-Reformation was successful in bolstering Catholicism in Southern Europe without further loss, and Northern Europe was stanched off by Catholic reforms in Ireland to be discussed in detail at another time.

---

[97] Ibid. MacCulloch, pg. 400.

Beckett, John. *The Glorious Revolution, Parliament, and the Making of the First Industrial Nation*. Parliamentary History: Wiley-Blackwell, 33, 1 (February 2014): 36-53.

Beddard, Robert. *Anti-Popery and the London Mob, 1688*. History Today: 38, 7 (July 1988): 36.

Boorstin, Daniel J. *The Discoverers*. New York, Random House (1985): 256.

Burke, Peter. *Jack Goody and the Comparative History of Renaissances*. Theory Culture and Society: 26, 16 (2009): 20, 22.

Carlton, Genevieve. *Worldly Consumers: The Demand for Maps in Renaissance Italy*. Ph. D. diss. Northwestern University (2011): 3.

Clifton, Robin. *James II's Two Rebellions*. History Today: 38, 7 (July 1988): 23-30.

Colman, Clark Stuart. *The Glorious Revolution of 1688 in Cumberland and Westmorland: The Merit of this Action*. Northern History: 40, 2 (September 2003): 237-259.

Encyclopaedia Britannica Online, "Glorious Revolution", last modified May 9, 2016, https://www.britannica.com/event/Glorious-Revolution

Encyclopaedia Britannica Online, "European Law," last modified June 19, 2008, https://www.britannica.com/topic/European-law

Eskridge III, Charles R. *Modern Lessons from Original Steps Towards the American Bill of Rights*. Texas Review of Law & Politics: 19, 1 (Fall of 2014): 25-62.

Gibson, William. *Dissenters, Anglicans and the Glorious Revolution: The Collection of Cases*. Seventeenth Century: 22, 1 (Spring of 2007): 168-184.

Goldie, Mark. *The Bill of Rights, 1689 and 1998*. History Today: 48, 9 (September 1998): 10-12.

Joliffe, John. *Bishop Ken and the Non-Jurors*. History Today: 65, 4 (April 2015): 47-52.

Key, Newton. *The "Boast of Antiquity": Pulpit Politics Across the Atlantic Archipelago during the Revolution of 1688*. Church History: 83, 3 (September 2014): 618-649.

Lock, Geoffrey. *The 1689 Bill of Rights*. Political Studies: 37, 4 (December 1989): 540-561.

Macculloch, Diarmaid. *The Reformation, A History*. New York: Penguin (2003): 10, 13, 15, 38, 65, 77, 78, 158, 198, 199, 400, 486, 500.

O'Neill, Jonathan. *Property Rights and the American Founding: An Overview*. Journal of Supreme Court History: 38, 3 (2013): 309-329.

Patterson, W. Brown. *The Glorious Revolution Reconceived*. Sewanee Review: 119, 2 (Spring 2011): 330-333.

Pesante, Maria Luisa. *Paradigms in English Political Economy: Interregnum to Glorious Revolution*. European Journal of the History of Economic Thought: 3, 3 (Autumn of 1996): 353-379.

Pincus, Steven. *A Fight for the Future*. History Today: 59, 10 (October 2009): 10-16.

Pfiffner, James P. *The Contemporary Presidency: Magna Carta and the Contemporary Presidency*. Presidential Studies Quarterly: 46, 1 (March 2016): 140-157.

Potter, Harry. *Liberty and the Common Law*. History Today: 65, 12 (December 2015): 19-24.

Speck, Bill. *Religion's Role in the Glorious Revolution*. History Today: 38, 7 (July 1988): 30-35.

Szechi, Daniel. *A Non-Resisting, Passively Obedient Revolution: Lord North and Grey and the Tory Response to the Sacheverell Impeachment*. Parliamentary History, Wiley-Blackwell: 31, 1 (February 2012): 118-127.

Vallance, Ted. *The Unrevolutionary Revolution? Interpreting the Revolution of 1688*. Teaching History: 151 (Jun, 2013): 18-19.

van Caenegem, R.C. *The Modernity of Medieval Law*. Legal History Review: 68, 3 (September 2000): 313-329.

Wootton, David. *John Locke and Richard Ashcraft's Revolutionary Politics*. Political Studies: 40, 1 (March 1992): 79-98.

Zook, Melinda S. *The Restoration Remembered: The First Whigs and the Making of their History*. Seventeenth Century: 17, 2 (Autumn of 2002): 213-235.

Chapter VI

English Law Principles, the Bill of Rights of 1689, and Their Impact on the American Framers and the U.S. Constitution

Historiography

Introduction

The United States Constitution was deeply influenced by England's legal and philosophical foundations, including English common law and the Bill of Rights of 1689. The Founders sought to remedy the abuses of the British Crown and Parliament by building safeguards directly into the supreme law of the new nation: the Constitution, which is ironically modeled in part after England's uncodified constitution.

In addition to the Bill of Rights of 1689, the United States Constitution contains other significant legal advancements throughout England's history, such as the *Magna Carta* of 1215 CE (which allowed for greater power-sharing between the Crown and barons), the Petition of Right of 1628 CE (also establishing rights that the Crown cannot impinge), and the *Habeas Corpus* Parliament of 1679 CE (which established required proof for lawful imprisonment; also found in Article 1, Section 9 of the U.S. Constitution). This combination of laws and legal practices are known as English common law.

1. The Principles of English Common Law

English common law was developed over many years, beginning with the importation of Roman law and locally developed by its earliest lawgivers. As stated above, important developments followed in laws requiring increased royal power-sharing and the recognition of the barons' rights, as in the *Magna Carta* which attempted to limit the arbitrary rulings of the English monarchs. These themes continued throughout England's history, leading to the Glorious Revolution of 1688 and the institution of the British Bill of Rights in 1689 and its subsequent constitution.

With the advent of the Age of Enlightenment, legal philosophies changed. By the end of the 17th century, the idea of natural rights permeated Enlightenment-age philosophy and found its way into the legal concepts of human rights, self-evident and unalienable rights of humanity that were not provided by any person, sovereign or legal system, but are universal and freely inherent within human existence.

Later, popular revolutions in America and France fueled even greater changes to legal practices. Philosophical leaders in this area were John Locke (1632-1704 CE) and Thomas Hobbes (1588-1679 CE), who wrote extensively on the natural rights of man, classical republicanism and liberal theory, which drove the parliamentary process in England.

According to Potter, "The common law of England has been compared to a broad river with many tributaries or to a tree with many deep roots and myriad branches…its authority depends on its antiquity, on its ability to change and on popular involvement and public acceptability."[98] Britain's population is a study in tribal conquests and transformation. First, the Anglo-Saxons replaced the Britons. The Vikings wreaked havoc along England's shores and applied *Dane law*. Lastly, the Normans, under William the Conqueror, unified England in the 11th century; but it was under Henry II (1133-1189 CE) that common law coalesced.[99]

Prior to this, there existed separate, uncoordinated legal systems. Henry II led the reform of England's legal system, which included the amassing of power for the throne. Despite this, throughout the 12th and 13th centuries, England's system of courts became more uniform; judges and lawyers were trained effectively in common law and the jury system was retained. It was these reforms that proved their worth and ultimately led to the curtailing of royal power through the *Magna Carta* in 1215 CE.

The promotion and support of the jury system has many valuable features that make commoners key to the system of justice. It quelled violence between parties and reduced vigilantism. Juries replaced the posse where vengeance was transformed into justice. This is a significant transfer of historical power from God, kings and bureaucrats to the people - the beginning of a revolutionary age for the common man. This was a departure from continental European states which still employed older forms of justice not necessarily invested in the people. England's

---

[98] Harry Potter, *Liberty and the Common Law*, (History Today: 65, 12 (December 2015), 19.
[99] Encyclopaedia Britannica Online, *European Law*, last modified June 19, 2008, https://www.britannica.com/topic/European-law

legal system of common law continued to develop through the Middle Ages and the Early Modern Period.[100]

2. The Bill of Rights of 1689

The Bill of Rights of 1689 CE was an Act of Parliament that declared specific limits to the powers of the monarchy and empowered the Parliament with additional rights not to be infringed by the Crown. It held that the Parliament should meet regularly, hold free elections, be protected while in Parliament, protected freedom of speech and outlawed cruel and unusual punishment.

The Bill of Rights of 1689 CE is the culmination of many years of England's social changes and the consistent drive of its leaders, both religious and secular, to maintain moral and legal justification for its actions. Nobles and preachers pointed to British history to explain the events of the Glorious Revolution. According to Key, "Preachers…used occasional or state sermons to explain contemporary upheavals from the perspective of God's law, Natural law, and Civil law."[101]   Britain established the Bill of Rights in 1689 CE to restrict the monarchy from indiscriminate power and invest more sovereignty with the Parliament and the people.   The Bill of Rights of 1689 CE is the bedrock of the British constitution and five out of thirteen Articles are still in use today.

3. The Foundation of Law in the Early United States

By 1770 CE, less than one century after the Glorious Revolution, the Thirteen American Colonies were faced with very similar circumstances. From the American Colonies' perspective, Britain abused its power, levied burdensome taxes and the Colonies had no legal rights to represent themselves. Try as they might, the Colonies were unsuccessful in influencing King George III (1738-1820 CE) or Parliament and their opposition was met with force at the Boston Massacre, where American

---

[100] Encyclopaedia Britannica Online, *European Law*, last modified June 19, 2008, https://www.britannica.com/topic/European-law
[101] Newton Key, *The "Boast of Antiquity": Pulpit Politics Across the Atlantic Archipelago during the Revolution of 1688*, (Church History: 83, 3 (September, 2014), 618.

colonial civilians were killed by British soldiers. This event began a period that led to the American War for Independence, or Revolutionary War. The Founders of the United States of America made monumental efforts to provide a sound legal footing for the rebellion against Britain. From this is derived the great charters of America's founding: the Declaration of Independence in 1776 CE, the Articles of Confederation in 1781 and the United States Constitution and the Bill of Rights in 1789 CE, exactly 100 years after the Glorious Revolution.

The leaders of the American Colonies were not simply revolutionaries rejecting the yoke of an oppressive Old World monarchy, but were legal scholars - learned men of letters and Enlightenment philosophy - and, as such, were indisputably the Framers of the legal principles and Founders of construct of the United States of America.

According to Patrick, the uncodified English constitutional agreements were the framework and basis for the U.S. Constitution. He discerns: "The three charters [*Magna Carta,* 1628 Petition of Rights and 1689 Bill of Rights] were legal limitations on the power of the English monarchy that eventually tilted the balance of power in government toward the Parliament, the representatives of the people. Limits on the monarch's power were accompanied by recognition of the Parliament's power and the people's rights in written documents. These rights of Englishmen were carried to North America in colonial charters issued by the Crown."[102]

The American Colonies had a long history of modeling English law well prior to the Revolutionary War. In 1641 CE, the Massachusetts Body of Liberties was the first legal charter of its kind established in the Colonies. While it was repudiated by the Crown in 1684 CE, it formed the basis for the later Bill of Rights, having such components as due process, freedom of speech, jury trial, just punishment, bail, compensation for property confiscation and double jeopardy. During the 1600s, many other states within the colonies also had similar charters, including: Maryland, Rhode Island, Connecticut, New Hampshire, Pennsylvania and New York. What made the American legal perspective so unique is that they attempted to check power in all branches of

---

[102] John J. Patrick, *The Roots of American Rights* (Oxford: Oxford University Press, 2003), 15.

government, not simply the Crown as did England. Patrick explains, "These colonial American documents guaranteed the rights of individuals through limitations on all branches of the government. By contrast, the 17th-century English documents on rights expressed limitations only against the monarchy on behalf of Parliament."[103] These distinctions played out forcefully in the years leading to the Revolution and after in the drafting of the Constitution.

4. The Revolution

During the prewar years, the English Crown and Parliament treated the Colonies as more or less property of England, while being somewhat permissive with local laws; however, once England decided on a course, local laws were summarily disregarded as evidenced in the passage of several Acts of Parliament that led to the Revolution. The Revolution was sparked by a blatant disregard for local representation, especially on taxes which were a right offered to the British under the 1689 English Bill of Rights. The Colonies had no representation in Parliament and were on the receiving end of dictates by Parliament and the Crown. A series of reforms were proposed during the years prior to the Revolution without success. During the 1760s and 1770s, Parliament passed several Acts that had a damaging effect on American commerce, leading the Colonies to revolt against England. During the Revolution, England committed what we legally interpret today and what was certainly viewed by the colonists then, to be illegal and, therefore, criminal acts. The British police forces often violated the law, dashing any expectations for justice by the colonists. With general warrants, homes were raided and often people were hauled off to jail without probable cause. This concern was very important to the colonists. In fact, according to Monk, "After the Revolutionary War, eight states prohibited general warrants in their constitutions."[104]

Based on Enlightenment philosophy, specifically the work of Locke, in the minds of the colonists and especially those of the Founders; it was

---

[103] Ibid. Patrick, pg. 18.
[104] Linda R. Monk, *The Words We Live By, Your Annotated Guide To The Constitution* (New York, Boston: Stonesong Press, 2015), 162.

human beings that brought 'natural law' into governmental and societal organizations which cannot be established or revoked by a monarch, government or political body. So, when Parliament issued the series of economically adverse taxes in the late 1700s, the colonists balked. The Stamp Act of 1765 CE and the Townshend Act of 1767 CE were taxes issued by Parliament to the Colonies, which placed constraints on colonial commerce and fueled the negative perception that Parliament did not consider local concerns before issuing taxes. When the Colonies resisted, Parliament placated the Colonies by reducing the amount of taxes required, but in retribution, Parliament also issued the Declaratory Act of 1766 CE which stated, in no uncertain terms, that Parliament had the unilateral right to levy taxes on the Colonies without their consent. This is largely due to the fact that after 1689 CE, Parliament became supreme in England after its confrontation with the Crown and the colonial resistance was perceived as a threat to their supremacy. Nonetheless, this Act further infuriated the Colonies.

In 1773 CE, Parliament passed the Tea Act which quickly led to the Boston Tea Party. Led by Samuel Adams (1722 – 1803 CE), a Founder and statesman, the Boston Tea Party was an act of public resistance to England's taxes on the colonies. The participants dumped an entire shipment of tea into Boston Harbor under the guise of Native Americans. Parliament retaliated by issuing the Intolerable Acts in 1774 CE. This group of Acts punished the Colonies by distributing restrictive powers to the Crown and local governors to enforce English law over colonial law. They suspended many of the freedoms enjoyed by the colonies, including due process, unlawful search and seizure and allowed the quartering of British troops. The Massachusetts Charter was revoked, sparking mass outrage. With greater resistance, Parliament became more inflexible. Settlement between England and the Colonies became unachievable. All of these actions by England provided the necessary footing for the Founders to build a legal justification for revolution and ultimately independence from Britain.

Leaders across the Colonies rallied in support of the Massachusetts Colony. Patrick relays that, "In September 1774, the First Continental Congress met in Philadelphia to decide what the colonies should do to oppose the British. Representatives came from every colony except

Georgia. This body passed the *Declaration and Resolves* of the Continental Congress to express American opposition to violations of individual rights in the colonies."[105]

Resistance to England quickly escalated after the meeting of the Continental Congress. A militia was formed in each of the colonies and opposition measures were coordinated. Militia soldiers were called Minutemen, because they would rally in a minute's call. The pressure between the Colonies and Britain exploded on April 19, 1775, when the local militia was challenged by British troops in Lexington, Massachusetts. At the standoff, a gun was discharged and a short battle ensued, leaving eight colonists dead and one British soldier wounded. This was the final of several flashpoints that instigated the Revolutionary War. Soon after the conflicts at Lexington and Concord on May 10, 1775, the Colonies met again in Philadelphia as the Second Continental Congress to discuss independence from Britain.

The Founders were abundantly aware that the resistance movement and direct conflicts with the British army would inevitably lead to war. In order to prepare, the Colonies selected their best representatives to send to Philadelphia at the Second Continental Congress, but simply coordinating efforts as was done by the First Continental Congress was not enough. So, in May, 1776, the 'united states in Congress assembled' (as the new government was soon called), proposed and sought ratification of America's first constitution: the Articles of Confederation. Their full name was the *Articles of Confederation and Perpetual Union*, because unity was the most critical prerequisite if the Colonies were to win their independence from Great Britain.

Prior to this, the First Continental Congress had issued to Parliament its *Declaration and Resolves*, which outlined the Colonies' grievances against England due to the Intolerable Acts and stated that the Colonies would boycott such unreasonable demands unless redress occurred. A petition was issued to the King of England as well, requesting repeal of the Tax Acts. This was an attempt to secure the proper rights of British subjects. Both were rebuffed.

The Second Continental Congress issued to Parliament its *Declaration of the Causes and Necessity to Take Up Arms*, which

---

[105] Ibid. Patrick, pg. 38.

explained why the Colonies found it necessary to formally contest England. It cited the admiralty courts which violated due process and underscored the Colonies' vociferous objection to taxation without local representation. It also pointed out the injustice of England's aggressiveness by sending troops and enforcing unilateral coercive laws designed to suppress what the Colonies perceived as just grievances. This overture was also rejected by Parliament and the Crown. An escalation of fractiousness is clearly found in the declarations between the First and Second Continental Congresses, but also found is the ongoing development of colonial law.

In July of 1776 CE, these steps culminated in the Declaration of Independence. Ironically, the progress made through the efforts of the First and Second Continental Congresses prepared the Colonies for not only its fight for independence but arranged the building blocks for a republican constitutional government. Swindler observes:

"These resolutions in themselves marked a transitional step in American constitutional thought. The famous Declaration of Independence, which followed in July, was actually the third in a series of declarations by the Continental Congress…in order to secure their rights as Englishmen; the English colonists now declared that they had to be independent of England itself."[106]

This is a critical understanding of the mindset of the American colonists. As previously noted, they professed human rights as independent of government or monarchy and attempted to reconcile this with England's forcible escalations. According to natural law, England's own actions provided the legal justification for independence. The Congress needed to devise a more comprehensive charter to substantiate its ideas and activities. It did so with the Articles of Confederation.

5. The United States Constitution

Under the Articles of Confederation, the Continental Congress named their new alliance, "The United States of America." In total, the document stated thirteen articles with which the Colonies unanimously

---

[106] William F. Swindler, *Our First Constitution: The Articles of Confederation*, (American Bar Association Journal: 67, 2, February of 81), 166.

agreed. Essential foundations contained in the Articles include: state sovereignty, ability to conduct war, an attack on one state is an attack on all, one vote per state; it retained enumerated powers to Congress, established funding mechanisms and maintained that Congress was the sole authority to amend its responsibilities. These were all critical functions in order to fund, operate and prosecute a war. Once the Revolutionary War was won, however, the Articles were not robust enough to manage the new nation. The Articles were limited in scope and could not amply sustain the union of the colonies. Consequently, the Founders sought a clearer and more comprehensive constitution. The Articles remained in force from 1781 CE to 1789 CE, when they were replaced by the United States Constitution.

While America was independent things were not progressing well. Berkin states, "Dark clouds and a suffocating gloom seemed to have settled over the country, and these men understood that something had gone terribly wrong."[107] Many framers of the Articles of Confederation and the generation of lawyers, political scientists and thinkers that followed noted in dismay the shortcomings that the loose compact of the Articles was failing. The flaws of the Articles culminated in August, 1786, with Shays' Rebellion in Massachusetts. 1,500 farmers deeply frightened by foreclosures, lack of credit and debt took up arms and marched on Springfield, Massachusetts, and commandeered the courthouse. Daniel Shays was a Revolutionary War veteran of the Battle of Saratoga. This event starkly revealed that something significant had to be done to better lead and organize the thirteen states.

In addition, the fledgling United States was on the receiving end of several diplomatic humiliations, an inability to expand economically and protect its interests abroad. Shipping lines were disrupted, credit was overextended and it had no effective central government to remedy these challenges. The Articles served well enough during the Revolution, but its inadequacies became abundantly clear in the years following. The challenge would be to move from the Articles, which roughly held thirteen states together for a single purpose, to a central form of government that honored states' rights, but had the power to address

---

[107] Carol Berkin, *A Brilliant Solution, Inventing the American Constitution* (New York: Mariner Books, 2002), 11.

challenges and solutions as one nation. Berkin says it this way: "The Continental Congress showed little inclination to 'think continentally' as they wrote the Articles of Confederation."[108]

With John Adams and Thomas Jefferson in Europe performing their state duties, others needed to assume the responsibility of framing this new blueprint. Adams and Jefferson had individually penned some of the greatest works of the Revolution: Jefferson's Declaration of Independence and Adam's Massachusetts' Constitution. With this background considered, the Constitution is remarkable in several ways and totally unique in the advancement of a representative republic with democratic principles.

The Constitution, in its three main Articles, invested the power of legislating laws to the Congress made up of state representatives and the Senate. The president, as chief executive, was removed from legislative activities, curtailing the power of the office, but was granted the ability to sign laws or veto approval. The judiciary, appointed by the president and confirmed by the Senate, would act independently from Congress and the president. This arrangement was purposely designed in contrast to the abuses of Britain's monarchy and Parliament. We know this as the 'separation of powers' so critical to the foundation of the Constitution. Further, the Congressional Oath of Office required one's sacred honor to be invested in any passage of laws, making it a personal achievement which had the effect of ensuring sensible, honorable laws. This with several other smart rules like age requirements, prevented nepotism; no requirement for land ownership or tax payment made it possible for any citizen to participate in government.

British self-governance long struggled for against the Crown culminated in the Bill of Rights in 1689, but England still remained an elite governmental structure that relied on wealthy barons in both the Houses of Lords and Commons which was hardly republican, and the king had the power to dissolve assembled government bodies on a whim. Royal governors of the colonies also had this authority vested in their office. The Founders viewed this as direct contradictions to popular sovereignty. According to Amar, the Founders, "...went several steps

---

[108] Ibid. Berkin, pg. 18.

beyond ancient republics and the British constitution."[109] In 1787 CE, the colonies empowered a Constitutional Convention in Philadelphia to draft a new United States constitution. Key participants included James Madison who was charged with its outline, Alexander Hamilton, Benjamin Franklin, Robert Morris, George Washington, Gouverneur Morris, Charles Pinckney and 35 others who ultimately signed the Constitution that summer.

Within the convention's ranks were opposing cliques holding certain philosophies of government. We identify these opposing cliques as Federalists and Anti-Federalists. The Federalists were proponents of a loose, decentralized form of government in keeping with their revolutionary and republican principles, but believed the Articles of Confederation were too weak and a stronger central or federal government was required. Catalysts in this group were James Madison, who often penned the Federalist Papers, and Alexander Hamilton. The Anti-Federalists opposed the ratification of the Constitution and were represented by Thomas Jefferson, James Monroe and George Mason. The Anti-Federalists worried that a strong federal government would lead to the same abuses of the British monarchy and Parliament. Their influence led to the passage of the Bill of Rights, consisting of the first ten Amendments to the Constitution due to the Massachusetts Compromise. The Federalists, after the Massachusetts Compromise, essentially got the stronger federal government they wanted and what we now live with today.

6. Conclusion

What these events bear out is that despite monumental historical trials from monarchs, militaries and social upheavals, British common law has endured because of the application of the 'rule of law' and 'due process' of the law, found in major historical junctures like the Glorious Revolution. From there, Western Civilization has spread its concepts of limited government, human freedom and equality. Certainly, it is an ideal that human beings are at their best when they are free, which has

---

[109] Akhil Reed Amar, *America's Constitution, A Biography* (New York: Random House Trade Paperbacks, 2005), 13.

prevailed only at certain times and in some societies throughout the ages. It is the concepts of natural law, human rights, equality, fair representation and, ultimately, the freedom of humanity that are vital steps in the progress of Western society and humanity. It is these notions that inspired the *Magna Carta*, the English Glorious Revolution of 1688 CE, the Declaration of Independence and the United States Constitution. Human freedom, in its best times, has faced down tyranny and opened the human spirit to unprecedented creativity and the triumph of law. In freedom's absence history tells of slavery, servitude, arrested development and arbitrary governance.

The passage of the Constitution rested upon the monumental yet difficult work already accomplished in the American Colonies' brief but rich history since its founding through the declarations under the Continental Congress and the ratification of the Articles of Confederation. Several factors had the potential to stand in the way of accomplishing any one of these major feats: state sovereignty, equal representation regardless of population or geographic size, fear of the abuse of power, demands for codifying human rights, legitimate debates on the optimal composition of a legislative, executive and judicial government funding, security, recognition by foreign governments and several others. Despite this, the Framers and Founders remained engaged, debated and devised solutions.

This stands in stark contrast to what we're witnessing in government today. The issues are no less important, impact all citizens and have deep effects on American life. The Founders' engagement was illuminated by the philosophies and legal practices throughout Western civilization. They had a drive inspired by the democracies of ancient Greece, the power-sharing of the *Magna Carta* and the parliamentary government that took root in Enlightenment Europe culminating with the English Bill of Rights of 1689. This drive produced our great American legal heritage and the beginning of a new nation; the United States of America.

Chapter VI - Works Cited and Consulted

Amar, Akhil Reed. *America's Constitution, A Biography*. New York: Random House Trade Paperbacks, 2005.

Berkin, Carol. *A Brilliant Solution, Inventing the American Constitution*. Boston, New York: Mariner Books, 2003.

Encyclopaedia Britannica Online. "Glorious Revolution," last modified May 9, 2016. https://www.britannica.com/event/Glorious-Revolution

Encyclopaedia Britannica Online. "European Law," last modified June 19, 2008. https://www.britannica.com/topic/European-law

Eskridge III, Charles R. *Modern Lessons from Original Steps Towards the American Bill of Rights*. Texas Review of Law & Politics: 19, 1 (Fall 2014): 25-62.

Goldie, Mark. *The Bill of Rights, 1689 and 1998*. History Today: 48, 9 (September 1998): 10-12.

Key, Newton. *The "Boast of Antiquity": Pulpit Politics Across the Atlantic Archipelago during the Revolution of 1688*. Church History: 83, 3 (September 2014): 618-649.

Lock, Geoffrey. *The 1689 Bill of Rights*. Political Studies: 37, 4 (December 1989): 540-561.

Monk, Linda R. *The Words We Live By, Your Annotated Guide To The Constitution*. New York, Boston: Stonesong Press, 2015.

Patrick, John J. *The Roots of American Rights*. Oxford: Oxford University Press, 2003.

Patterson, W. Brown. *The Glorious Revolution Reconceived*. Sewanee Review: 119, 2 (Spring 2011): 330-333.

Pincus, Steven. *A Fight for the Future*. History Today: 59, 10 (October 2009): 10-16.

Pfiffner, James P. *The Contemporary Presidency: Magna Carta and the Contemporary Presidency*. Presidential Studies Quarterly: 46, 1 (March 2016): 140-157.

Potter, Harry. *Liberty and the Common Law*. History Today: 65, 12 (December 2015): 19-24.

Swindler, William F. *Our First Constitution: The Articles of Confederation*. American Bar Association Journal: 67, 2 (February 81): 166-170.

Szechi, Daniel. *A Non-Resisting, Passively Obedient Revolution: Lord North and Grey and the Tory Response to the Sacheverell Impeachment*. Parliamentary History (Wiley-Blackwell): 31, 1 (February 2012): 118-127.

Vallance, Ted. *The Unrevolutionary Revolution? Interpreting the Revolution of 1688*. Teaching History: 151 (June 2013): 18-19.

Wootton, David. *John Locke and Richard Ashcraft's Revolutionary Politics*. Political Studies: 40, 1 (March 1992): 79-98.

About the Author

Joseph DiRienzo (M.A.) has his undergraduate and graduate degrees in History, with a focus on Ancient and Classical studies and American History. Joseph's passion is to make history digestible and relevant to modern readers. This is the author's first book, but he is looking forward to undertaking other interesting historical subjects to share with his readers. In addition to history, Joseph enjoys philosophy, sociology, psychology and religious studies.

It is his hope that you enjoy this book and that it inspires your own interest in the rich history and contributions of Western Civilization.

Joseph can be contacted at joediro@optimum.net.

Made in the USA
Middletown, DE
07 March 2020

86013074R00095